# BEYOND CYNICISM
## The Practice of Hope

# Beyond Cynicism

## THE PRACTICE OF HOPE

by
DAVID O. WOODYARD

THE WESTMINSTER PRESS
Philadelphia

*Book design by Dorothy Alden Smith*

Published by The Westminster Press ®
Philadelphia, Pennsylvania

PRINTED IN THE UNITED STATES OF AMERICA

---

Library of Congress Cataloging in Publication Data

Woodyard, David O.
   Beyond cynicism.

   Includes bibliographical references.
   1. Hope. I. Title.
BV4638.W66          234′.2          75-190504
ISBN 0-664-20942-4 (Cloth)
ISBN 0-664-24961-2 (Paper)

To
PAUL L. BENNETT

whose loyalty to the future
has nurtured hope
in generations of his students

# CONTENTS

# PREFACE

Sometimes a person writes a book because he wants to; sometimes because he has to. Perhaps the difference is in the degree to which an author's existence is demanding a more precise statement of where he is and why he is there. I have felt driven in the preparation of this manuscript, not by a surge of originality, but by a need to articulate my faith in relation to a pervasive cynicism about the prospects of a new future. It seems an especially compelling time in which to affirm one's belief in God and the church as they pertain to the prospects of social change. Some may thrive on the death of one and the deterioration of the other. But others of us are finding confidence in understanding God as the power of the future and the church as a community of hope.

In the preparation of a manuscript an author has many debts beyond those persons who have influenced his thought. I have been privileged to serve under two college presidents, the late A. Blair Knapp and Joel P. Smith, who have encouraged the flexibility in responsibilities that has provided time to write. Two colleagues, William W. Nichols and David A. Gibbons, read the first draft and made insightful and demanding criticisms. The burden of writing has been lessened by the competent and cheerful assistance of Mrs. Robert E. Davis, who typed early drafts, and Betty Apollonio, who prepared the final manuscript.

It is a subthesis of this study that freedom for the future is a function of the sociopolitical realities within which men's lives are enmeshed. One institution, apart from the church, has been especially prominent in my own experience of hope and nurture in freedom. It is the family. Both the home of my birth and the home created by marriage have been "institutions" within which I have received and celebrated the gifts of the future. There the viability of practicing hope has been confirmed daily and durably. Thus one can say, "As for me and my house, we will serve the Lord" (Josh. 24:15).

D. O. W.

*Denison University*
*Granville, Ohio*

# INTRODUCTION

There is always a distinctive context from within which we approach the Christian message. For many of us in the 1970's it is the struggle to live beyond cynicism. By cynicism I mean being distrustful of institutions and their capacity to change, disaffected with individuals and their unwillingness to transcend self-interest, contemptuous of the good that can come of man and society, and in general pessimistic about the possibilities for the future. Having felt the pain and anguish of the age, we are tempted to conclude that very little can be done about it. It is not long before inertia becomes a way of life and all the dynamism of existence is extinguished. For the man who aspires to understand himself and the world theologically, the prevailing threat does not come from guilt over his behavior, challenges from an empirically oriented culture, or even existential doubt. The threat is futurelessness, the contention that nothing will ever be appreciably different from what it now is. What we have to resist in ourselves is the conclusion that a viable future is inaccessible to us. It does not enhance our mood to be reminded that cynicism is a luxury we can ill afford; something that tends to make us more cynical! Our lives call for a vision of reality and a sense of what is real that will enable us to deny the self-indulgent dimensions of cynicism and affirm life once again.

To recall where many of us have been, theologically, in recent years only serves to accent the burden. We have moved abruptly from "getting the faith straight" to "setting the world straight." In the first phase we concentrated on extricating our understanding of Christianity from cultural pollutants. The intent was to restore authenticity through a rigorously Biblical theology. For many of us, there emerged substantial confidence that we knew what our faith was all about. That this occurred during a religious revival of sorts obscured the fact that the people in the churches were not with us. The strange new world of the Bible remained remarkably alien and impenetrable. The end of the revival exposed the soliloquies in which we had been involved. We may have found the gospel but we lost the world in which it was to be heard.

It was probably the swift developments within the early civil rights movement that transported many of us into the second phase. We left our studies for the streets. Seminary students who in former times had written tedious papers on "the world come of age" now aspired to a piece of the maturation themselves. We had a sense of where we ought to be and felt right when we were there. When men like Roger Hazelton observed that we were deeply and rightly involved in civil rights without a theology of involvement, it passed us by as an interesting but not devastating comment. To be where the action is has its numbing exhilaration. The questions of whose actions these were and the criteria for involvement did not surface forcefully. And to have a constituency, even if it seldom overlapped with our congregations, was indeed a good feeling. Some indulged their members on Sunday mornings and supplied a few pastoral calls during the week so that they would be free to be involved with more important matters.

But the abrupt shifting of gears from "getting the faith straight" to "setting the world straight" left many of us with feelings of uneasiness. Theological slogans emerged like "Christian presence in the world," but they did not finally explain or sustain what we were about. Some gave up on that count—left the ministry, opted for the death of God, or formed new communities. But for others of us something in the nature of a conversion experience occurred. As our commitments in the world became more strenuous, the need became paramount for an understanding of the faith that would enable us to cope with the pain and anguish of the age. A dialectic of the streets and our studies began to emerge. We found we could not remain in the streets without having done our homework; nor could we, having done our homework, remain in our studies. Blacks kept saying to us, "Get yourselves together; check out where you are coming from." And it became important once again to understand ourselves theologically. That conversion experience was brought about largely by the threat of cynicism. With an enlarged consciousness that was on to the scope of the problems and society's resistance to change, we were suddenly up against the wall in a way we had not been before. For the first time we understood that the structures of death were not merely physical but social. The threats of nonbeing flaunted us in the forms of resistance to humanizing efforts. Goodwill and good efforts were not sufficient to bring about change. Violence became viable, thus marking the pinnacle of cynicism. We were suffocated with the sense of futurelessness.

As the exhilaration of action was played out, we found a need for a dynamism in our existence that could sustain the search for a viable future. Having tried purifying our understanding of faith and having shifted abruptly to acts of love, we felt the need to relate the two through the practice of hope. The theology of hope movement, popularly identified with Jürgen Moltmann, provided the needed theoretical constructs to cope with our incipient cynicism. But it seemed to say so little about what it would mean to live hope. That was focused for many on a spring night at Duke University during the first major conference of Americans with Moltmann. The word came into the auditorium that Martin Luther King had been assassinated. In the course of discussion Moltmann was asked what the theology of hope had to say to that. He replied, "I don't know. I'm not an American." There was something important and honest about that response. But for many of us it was the first awareness we had that the task for Americans was to discern what it means to practice hope.

It is the intent of this book to speak of hope with the phenomenon of cynicism in view. It is as persons struggling to overcome the feeling of futurelessness that we come to ask what the Christian faith has to say about hope. Our task is to find a basis for hope that enables us to live beyond the hopelessness engendered by present realities. That requires both a theory of hope and a notion of what it would mean to practice hope. It is not enough to identify the grounds of hope; one must also determine a manner in which it can be lived. While some of the chapters that follow are weighted more in one direction than the other, we are at all times concerned with hope as something that can be implemented.

In Chapter I we begin with the concern that the Christian faith has been mercilessly privatized. One reason it has not served us well in the streets is that it has been conceived primarily in interpersonal categories and applied to our individual lives. What we need is a radical deprivatizing of the gospel. The fissures and fractures of our humanity are not primarily private events but public ones. We are not so much restricted and deformed by our personal relations as by the structures, institutions, and mores that form our life in society. An understanding of the Christian faith that can unpack our cynicism is one that thrusts itself into the public arena.

This process of public hope is not alien to the nature of man. In Chapter II attention is given to man as the creature who hopes. He is most fully human when an anticipating consciousness is awakened and he lives from his visions rather than his memories of the past or the vicissitudes of the present. Cynicism is a distortion of man's disposition to hope; sin means to accept futurelessness and deny the possibilities of a radically new future. Man is authentic when he hopes militantly.

But in order for this to take place the tendency to sustain a linear view of history must be overcome. In Chapter III we strive to reverse the determination to think from the past through the present and then into the future. That sustains cynicism and deprives one of anticipating the decisively new in our lives. The alternative is to begin with the end, to give the future priority in our understanding of the past and present. Existence has a different quality when we begin with a sense of the openness of the future. Jesus' message of the coming Kingdom of God and his resurrection orient us away from what is or has been and toward the possibility of the unpredictable. To adequately sustain this perspective on our history demands an image of God in which he is interpreted as the power of the future activating the potentialities of the present. He is with us as the One who is ahead of us. When Moses asked for the name of God, his identity, Moses was told that God would be known to the Israelites in the events that were to come. As the God of the future, he brings us into the future. We know him as the radicality of possibilities in any moment.

When God is understood as the One who is before us now and always, his presence takes a peculiar form. In Chapter IV we explore the partiality of God. In Jesus of Nazareth it is made clear that God takes sides. He is not on the sidelines but a participant in the struggles of the oppressed against the oppressors. Man does not stand alone amid the pain and anguish of the world. The identification of God with those seeking time and space to be human is a wedge against cynicism. God aligns himself against the forces of futurelessness.

But to stand firm in that realization implicates one in the life of a community. In Chapter V the church is interpreted as a futuristic community. The people of God live beyond cynicism in mutual confirmation of the future. The life within the church is marked by rituals and relationships whereby men strengthen one another in hope. Prayer, preaching, and communion are all acts through which men orient themselves toward the coming reign of God. The practice of hope is thus nurtured in the church.

Christians, however, have to live as individuals, and that raises the issue of life-style. In Chapter VI we consider an understanding of the suffering of God in history as the point around which we fashion our lives. What this requires of us is the development of a proleptic life-style, living from anticipated conditions rather than those at hand. Those who get themselves together around the promises of God for a new future finally abort cynicism and are initiated into the limitless possibilities of every moment. That is the manner in which we give an account of the hope that is in us.

# I

# DEPRIVATIZING
# THE GOSPEL

One of the reasons the Christian faith has not sustained men at the intersection of their lives with sociopolitical realities is its pervasive alliance with the individual and personal as opposed to the public and institutional. Its vision and its verbiage have become predominantly interpersonal. The faith has been wedged into the lives of men at the point of their private struggles with death, guilt, and meaninglessness. It has focused upon the individual in his attempt to work out his own salvation as if his environment were not an integral part of the process. That we have nurtured this private form of the faith is reflected by the typical worshiper on Sunday morning, who comes with the expectation that he will find some word to get him through the week. His mind-set is that of an individual lobbying for relief rather than of a man in the midst of a community of men struggling with the forces of the social order that crush the spirit. If the word he hears in the sermon probes a social problem, he bemoans the fact that one cannot get anything spiritual in church anymore. He aspires to a private relationship with a personal God who will enable him to move through a social labyrinth but will not challenge its formation.

## The Public Context of Faith

An alternative would be to interpret the Christian message in the context of the social forces and institutional structures that affect our lives. Concern for the individual need not be expressed only in an individualistic way. It would be difficult to deny that the formation and deformation of our lives has distinctively interpersonal dimensions; subject-to-subject relationships are indeed significant. But the quality of our lives and the conditions of freedom are more often determined on broader terrain; we are more apt to be deprived of our possibilities as human beings by structures in the social order than by contacts in the realms of intimacy. It is significant that black Americans have shifted their attack from personal indignities, such as being called "boy," to institutionalized racism, such as zoning laws. Freedom for black human beings is a public event before it is a private one. When the structures in the social order work against a race, all the good human relations between the laundress and the lady of the house will not overcome the loss of humanity and the constriction of freedom.

It can be argued that a more effective way to be concerned with individuals is through the social setting of their lives. On the American frontier it may have been the case that individual initiative and virtue were the conditions essential to having life on one's own terms. Living toward one's own possibilities was a rather private affair. But now our destiny is more distinctly public in its formation and the sociopolitical realities are restrictive rather than supportive. Our lives are more directly determined by structures than by individuals; personal initiatives against them are often futile. A man cannot stand against social forces alone and with a faith that is allied primarily with the private dimensions of experience.

The consequence of this is that theology must find a new principle of interpretation, a new tool through which it wedges the gospel into our consciousness. We conclude that the search for understanding and the articulation of the faith must transpire in the context of our public life. Granted the complex social forces in the midst of which men now find themselves, it appears that the meaning of our faith will either be secured in our social existence or not at all. Those who persist in relating God to the private chambers of the soul have the effect of engendering practical atheism. The failure to formulate the faith and function with it under the conditions of society isolates its dynamic from the arena in which the decisions about our lives are really made. Of course, this does not mean giving religious sanction to particular political ideologies or movements; neither does it mean displacing theology with political concerns as if faith were an adjunct. But it does entail the development of a social consciousness in theology. The public rather than the private arena must be the dominant environment within which the faith is interpreted. To the degree that politics forms our destiny as persons, the Christian must take his stand there and make his faithful witness. Christians can live humanely only to the extent that they interpret the dangerous memory of Jesus and his message amid the conditions of contemporary society. That gospel exposes the coercions of the social order and draws the lives of men into a process of resistance to futurelessness.

Catholic theologian Johannes B. Metz draws the issue into focus somewhat negatively but in a way that highlights the problem. In our theological tradition there is what he calls "an extreme privatizing tendency" [1] that centers interpretation in the private rather than the public sector of our human experience. Classical theology has been formulated with assumptions and conceptions that anticipated no substantial tension between society and the life of faith. At best, the social consequences of faith were a second cousin in the theological enterprise. Sociopolitical realities were treated as relatively peripheral. To be sure, the individual Christian felt pressure from without, but he was not sustained by a faith in which a community of believers interpreted Christianity with the social order in view. The practice of faith tended to be reduced to the decision of the individual as he struggled with society. The community of faith was the place where he recovered his equilibrium. There the explication of the faith was intimate and private and related more to his fears and frustrations as a man than to the strangulation of his humanity by structures and institutions. The principle of interpretation traditionally has been apolitical. Obviously what this misses is the realization that man is deeply enmeshed in the vicissitudes of the social order.

What is needed is a deprivatizing of the gospel that, without denying the importance of the interpersonal, releases the faith for exposure to the public. The scale of the person is not broad enough to provide a base to interpret Christianity. To relate Christianity to the insular self without reference to the social matrix within which selfhood is formed and deformed is a failure to deal with problems on the levels at which they exist. The credibility of the faith for contemporary man will be determined by the measure in which it enables him to secure time and space to be human and to resist the coercions of his milieu, not by the measure in which it provides him with inner peace and personal security. The faith must be actualized within society so that the individual does not stand alone against it but in the power of a community of faith whose commitment to the future relativizes every present. While the specification of the faith in the public arena is the constructive task for theology in our time, "the deprivatizing of theology is the primary critical task." [2]

The distinctive assumption we are making about existence is that we only have our lives in some form of unit with other men. The transformations which really matter are in the midst of the company of men and affect decisively the organization of corporate existence. As Don Paolo says to Christina in Ignazio Silone's Bread and Wine: "I do not believe there is any way of saving one's soul today. He is saved who overcomes his individual egoism, family egoism, caste egoism, does not shut himself off in a cloister or build himself an ivory tower, or make a cleavage between his way of acting and his way of thinking. He is saved who frees his spirit from the idea of resignation to the existing disorder." [3] What is at issue is the way in which men stand together against the forces and structures which restrict their futures. Without a community of men, no man can stand against the forms of "existing disorder" that limit his destiny. Both oppression and liberation are functions of communities and the ways in which they are structured. And this is to affirm far more than the quality of interaction between persons. When one is concerned with the creation of a new history and the openness of the future, the issue of power is immediately raised. The negations of the inhuman and the affirmation of the humane involve one immediately in the exercise of power. The pursuit and practice of freedom in history are basically political in our time. The humane use of power in transcendence of the present conditions is the form freedom takes in our society. The vision of "a new heaven and a new earth" is activated through structures, institutions, and mores which are distinctively political in nature.

When James Cone identifies black power and the Christian message, there is a rather natural aversion to what he is saying in our white consciousness. Power is a dirty word, and to modify it with the adjective "black" only compounds the indemnity. The flaw in our response is not simply overlooking the implicit power in the white position but the consequences of powerlessness for black people. As an act of self-affirmation, black power is also the leverage to affect the conditions which dehumanize. "Black power, then, is a humanizing force because it is the black man's attempt to affirm his being, his attempt to be recognized as a 'thou' in spite of the 'other,' the white power which dehumanizes him." [4] Those who strive to live from a vision of a new future are concerned to possess the levers by which they can make room for the exercise of their freedom. And that is not first and foremost an inner event or attitude but a public or political process. The Christian, then, is not obsessed with achieving his personal salvation but with setting the conditions in society that will enable him and others to actualize their dreams. Salvation is not so much personal as it is institutional.

In Christian affirmations of the future, eschatology has been interpreted almost exclusively in relation to our personal destiny; but these affirmations connect with our public existence as well. Politics is the form that visions of the future take in the present order; and eschatological vision is the substance of political activity. While eschatology may well be more than politics, it dare not be less. If it fails to relate to the forms of power in society, it is restricted from influence amid the forces which inspirit or dispirit man. The coming Kingdom may not be a new bureaucracy, but it certainly intersects the bureaucracies which encapsulate the human spirit. Politics is dependent upon the Christian message about the future for the generation of its particular visions. It is the means by which a community of men implement their hopes; politics at best is hoping in action. But the genesis of the hopes is substantively related to the perspectives of faith. The resources of our faith must be utilized in relation to the world-changing processes in history through which man's spirit is enhanced or deflated. When God is understood as the power of the future, as we will develop in a later chapter, then he is related to the forces which open the future for man in the present and resist the structures of futurelessness. He connects with our lives at the points where we are being shaped and misshaped.

### Biblical Precedence

But what is the Biblical warrant for a public faith? The private dimensions are evident to us—and we would be dishonest to discredit them. The public context is generally more subtle, but nonetheless prevalent. Moses understood God as the One ahead of us calling man into the future on the strength of His promises. Standing before Pharaoh to demand freedom from the power structure was by any measure an act of faith. Awakened to the prospect of a new future, Moses challenged the present bondage of his people. It was not just piety but power which came into play. When Jesus proclaimed that the Kingdom was at hand and exhorted his hearers to repent and believe, his words went well beyond the personal dimension of existence. The claim was distinctively political in that it cut through the issue of who rules our lives. The proclamation of a coming Kingdom raises the issue of goverance by relativizing all the penultimate claims upon us. Indeed the rule of God directly calls in question our relationship with the powers that be in the social order. Jesus' message induces a man to check himself out politically. Paul clearly dwelt upon the sin of man, but he understood the forces external to man which distort his existence. While historically his words have reference to a gnostic dualism, in our time they identify structures as the enemy: "For we are not contending against flesh and blood, but against the principalities, against the powers, against the world rulers of this present darkness, against the spiritual hosts of wickedness in the heavenly places" (Eph. 6:12). The Biblical writers may not have been political analysts, but they articulated a faith which was both implicit and explicit in its application to the structures of the social order.

But the subtleties begin to surface at the point of translation. This becomes particularly evident when we consider the message of Jesus. It has to be acknowledged that the apparent intent of his ministry was an interior transformation, a change of heart in the lives of men. The manner in which he reset the focus of the Ten Commandments is evidence of his concern to bring about an inner revolution. We search the Gospels in vain for any steady or systematic treatment of the social and political consequences of this spiritual revolution. There is very little in the testimony of the early church that would support an image of Christ as a social activist or as one disposed to engage in power plays. While there is some evidence of a commitment to institutional reform, it tends to be subordinate to the conversion of the individual. But the conclusion to be drawn from this is not that it is illicit to develop a social consciousness within a theological perspective.

There are a number of reasons why the New Testament writers reflect a low profile in relation to the public context for interpreting the faith. It is not surprising that, to the degree that Jesus understood the Kingdom to be at hand, he was ill-disposed to make long-range political plans. Since the early church believed that the end was somewhat imminent, we should expect that the concentration would be more toward sensitizing people to the urgency of the hour than toward the formation of the social existence. One can argue as well that the tight political situation at the time of the early Christian church made it unlikely that anyone would be highly visible in protest. Existing as it did under a tyrannical power that felt threatened by any worldly allegiances other than to the emperor, the early church would tend to keep such political activity as there was secretive and underground. This, of course, is not to argue from silence that Jesus and his followers were really undercover agents whose primary intent was to subvert the system. It does suggest that we cannot expect an abundance of evidence for direct political action in the New Testament.

On the other hand, it would not be legitimate to say that Jesus was preoccupied with the conversion of individuals and indifferent to social reform. His ministry and message have dimensions that readily translate in the direction of the effect of social structures upon the quality of life he affirms for individuals. In time it became clear to the early church that justice in the social realm promoted the kinds of changes in the lives of individuals for which Jesus' message called. No lasting wedge can be lodged between the dynamics of personal conversion and the need for reform in the social structures. We will be most responsible to the needs of our age and to the Biblical witness if we sustain a reciprocal relationship between them. The process of living toward a future of one's own choosing requires a dialectic between the transformation of the individual and the transformation of the society in the midst of which his existence is acted out. There will be "no lasting political renewal without personal renewal, and no true personal renewal without political renewal." [5] The Biblical writings as a whole warrant that kind of relationship and they legitimate interpreting the faith in the direction of man's public as well as private existence.

### Antecedent Movements

We have been arguing for a principle of interpretation that leads to the development of what has been called a "political theology." We use the term to suggest a translation of the Christian message which has been weaned from the private dimensions of existence and oriented toward the sociopolitical realities of man's existence. It is prepared to draw out the meaning of Christianity for the ways in which the lives of men are affected by structures and institutions. Raising the question of whose world it is, a political theology is concerned with the possibilities for the future provided by social systems. It is a theology directed toward the use of power and its consequences for freedom. Indeed, it sees politics—as well as the private lives of men—as an area of God's activity.

A political theology is by no means the sole spokesman for the public dimension of the gospel in our century. Some will want to link it with the social gospel movement; a few suggest it is an unwitting rerun. The overlap is more apparent than real. Walter Rauschenbusch wrote in 1917: "The Kingdom ideal contains the revolutionary force of Christianity. . . . It translates theology from the static to the dynamic. . . . The Kingdom of God, at every stage of human development, tends toward a social order which will best guarantee to all personalities their freest and highest development. . . . [It] is not a concept nor an ideal merely, but an historical force. It is a vital and organizing energy now at work in humanity." [6] Certain words in that paragraph might suggest continuity. But a careful analysis of the thought content suggests discontinuity.

While the social gospel was developmental in its understanding of the Kingdom, a political theology understands the vitalizing force as coming from the future with the promise of a new event. The Kingdom does not emerge but intrudes. Rauschenbusch understood God as immanent in humanity urging the creation on to higher levels of achievement. In a sense, God is a property of history. For a political theology God is not within history but ahead of it. He calls man forward from before him rather than drives from within. God leads us out by awakening hope. As the power of the future he creates the present rather than evolves it. Rauschenbusch interpreted the Kingdom as operative at "every stage of human development"

and the social gospel as committed to redeeming the total social organism. Renewing and Christianizing the entire social
order were its goals. A political theology does not dissipate its
energies with concern for all the ills of society. It concentrates
upon the structures and institutions which restrict self-
determination and seeks to create ones which enable men to
get life going on their own terms. In this sense it is more limited in scope and more radical in intent; it zeroes in more nar-
rowly but with more demanding claims and expectations. And
the intent of a political theology is not to form a Christian civ-
ilization but to constitute the church as a community that util-
izes its power and perspective critically in relation to the structures of society. It is a misreading of a political theology to
suggest that it is a resuscitation of the social gospel. While the
latter was intent on redeeming social organisms, the former is
committed "to proclaim release to the captives, . . . to set at
liberty those who are oppressed" (Luke 4:18).

One of the obvious spin-offs of the social gospel was a syn-
thesis of religion and society, Christianity and social progress,
the gospel and a political ideology. The tension between
history and the Kingdom was dissolved. Reinhold Niebuhr
emerged in response to this distortion and provided an alternative version of Christianity interpreted in the social context.
While the social gospel rested on the naïve assumption that
love could be implemented in the structures of society, Niebuhr was a pragmatist and realist who looked for the approximations of love and justice which could be enacted in society.
Faith in the public arena meant realistic goals and pragmatic
tactics. Since man in his depraved state could not found the
Kingdom, his task was to implement here and there the approx-
imate claims of love. As far as man's efforts are concerned, the
Kingdom never comes, because the dilemmas of human existence are never resolved in history. But man can make some important adaptations.

Niebuhr's concept of the Kingdom made it a source of crisis
in history but never of fulfillment. It called in question the

conditions in the social order and held out a viable vision of love and justice. Yet when love is an impossible possibility, a goad rather than a goal, rather severe accommodations set in. It is at this point that a political theology is at odds with Niebuhr's political realism. "Niebuhrian realism gradually gave way to a complacent satisfaction with minimal expectations that all too easily supported the conservative *status quo*." [7] While Niebuhr disparages utopianism and affirms realism, a political theology affirms utopianism and disparages realism. A political theology, in understanding God as the power of the future effecting the present, refuses to reduce the demands of the Kingdom to the historically possible. Neither is it obsessed with the sense of ambiguity which tends to constrict the partiality of God in history. A political theology is prepared to risk judgments without forging long-range and irrevocable commitments. "Niebuhr does not adequately appreciate God's provisional identification with the powerless and the prostration of the powerful. . . . Niebuhr is too busy stressing the sinfulness of all men to acknowledge adequately the relative innocence of the powerless, oppressed, poor, and outcast." [8] Because a political theology fixes on the promises of God for a new creation, it makes bold to extend its reach beyond the possible. It is not known by the quality of its compromises but by the militancy of its hopes.

What a political theology aspires to create is an awareness of the tension between the promises of God for a new future and the sociopolitical realities of our lives. The gospel must stick to the social world as the locus of both judgment and assurance of hope. Its task is a critical response to social formations. The promises of peace, justice, liberation, and reconciliation conflict with and contradict present circumstances. The message of the Kingdom of God calls man into an involvement with world processes and a protest against all forms of futurelessness. To the extent that existence is a political problem, theology must engage in the attempt to formulate the Christian message politically. As Dietrich Bonhoeffer said during the days of Nazi oppression, "Only those who cry out for the Jews may sing Gregorian chants." Our interpretation of the faith must be transacted against its conflicts with man's public existence.

## Parameters

Now this practice of hope requires that we set some parameters. Without an estimate of the contours of responsibility, theology risks being dissolved into politics; without a vision of the imperative to public engagement, theology risks being dissolved into privatism. The first parameter is that the exercise of a political theology is an institutional task. This not only means that the church as a public institution has an obligation to develop in individuals a political consciousness, but that it as a body must act out that consciousness. The task of living from the promises of God cannot be left to individuals. The church has too often copped out with the assumption that its responsibility was simply to equip the saints for their tasks in the world. But the church is in the world as well and must prepare itself to respond to the promises of God as they are contradicted by futurelessness. This does not require it to forsake its commitments to the needs of individuals but to recognize that often the only way to minister to the individual is by affecting the structures and forces that shape his life. When evil is institutionalized, so must be the responses to it. It can be argued that some institutions are better equipped for power struggles than the church. Perhaps so. But the church is second to none in its vision of the future and the resources for social criticism. When the issue is oppression, what Paul Lehmann calls "the possibility of institutional counterpower" becomes both an option and an obligation.

There are those who argue that the church will be most effective if it acts by prophetic word rather than public deed. "The church, which calls itself the church of love, will be able to express a credible and efficient criticism of pure power only if, and to the extent that, it itself does not appear in the accouterments of power. The church cannot and must not desire to press its points by means of political power." [9] When the process of liberation is in focus, such purity is not an option for a community living from the future. Furthermore, the argument ignores the degree to which the church sanctions the present formation of power. The churches in America own one of the largest industrial investment portfolios in the nation; to the degree that they hold those investments uncritically, they are sanctioning political power. The argument of a political theology is that faith must be institutionalized; the church as a public institution is responsible for the promises of a new future in the message of Jesus as they are contradicted by the sociopolitical realities of the day. The community that sings Gregorian chants together is obligated to cry out for the Jews together.

The second parameter has to do with the provisional quality of identification in the world. In Chapter IV the partiality of God will be argued systematically. While the promises of hope are for all men, they are enacted through partisan identification. "Jesus' proclamation and deeds were valid for all men precisely because he took sides with the weak, the poor, and the victims of discrimination. Jesus grasped society, so to speak, at the lowest extreme, where he found the miserable and the disdained. Paul said the gospel is for all men, but he went onesidedly to the Gentiles in order to save the Jews." [10] God acts in the world through identification with the oppressed. The gospel is indeed "good news to the poor." And that risk of identification can be assumed because the oppressed have fewer options for the misuse of power. Powerlessness yields a position of relative purity. The occasions for exploitation are private and not public. Furthermore, as Cone argues, only the oppressed understand oppression; to that extent they are the key factors in liberation. One must be among the poor to know what it means to be excluded from wealth. One must experience hatred to understand the misery it creates. Those who cause those conditions, however well-intending in their charities, are remarkably oblivious to the suffering they inflict.

Yet for all that, the identification is provisional. The only ir-

revocable identification of God is in Christ. God is free to
switch sides. Assyria may become the instrument of his wrath
against his beloved Israel. The ease with which the oppressed
become oppressors is startling. It has been said that nothing is
more conservative than a revolutionary in power. While the goal
of the revolt of the oppressed may be elimination of the slave—
master relationship, the effect in fact may be no more than a
reversal of roles. Then while God remains partisan, he has
switched partners. The power of the future always aligns itself
with the forces of liberation but in a manner that is provisional. A political theology dare never translate into a civil religion in which the inquisitory spirit is domesticated and faith is
reduced to a social ritual by which a country assures itself of
sanctity. In fact, the task of a political theology is to desacralize
the presumptions of identification of God with the powerful.
To the degree that the Christian faith follows the crucified
one, it will be on the alert for all the graven images in the political order. When we note the provisional quality of identification, it is to be distinguished from divinization. God takes
sides, but he does not share divinity.

The third parameter of a political theology is that the Christian is not bound absolutely to utilize the systems of society or
the laws that support it. The future of God is not bound up
with the maintenance of existing institutions nor with their
use; indeed, systems and laws are relativized by the eschatological anticipations. It is the peculiar freedom of the Christian "to
support the given structures if they are fluid enough to grow in
service to all men, to change them when they block the coming
of a more just society, even to overthrow them with force when
the controlling powers have become insane and demonic." [11]
Those who would argue that the only form of responsible political response is "working through the system" are on faulty theological ground. Christians have been encapsulated by a few
Pauline references to the state and a misreading of Jesus'
remark about rendering unto Caesar. Acting against the systems and laws of society is a decision a Christian has the option of making, albeit reluctantly; love may call a man or his

community outside the boundaries of rationality and good form, setting him to the implementation of the future against the resistance of society's structures. It is rare in history that power has yielded its privileges in an orderly way. When the process won't respond, initiatives are called for that transcend normal limits. The seeking of justice, peace, and reconciliation cannot always be accomplished "within the system"; indeed, the systems may very well be institutionalized futurelessness. Then living outside the law may be the only form of lawfulness.

Daniel Berrigan, in a play he wrote about the trial of the Catonsville Nine, answers the question raised by the defense about the impact an illegal act of his brother had upon him:

> I began to understand
> one could not indefinitely obey the law
> while social institutions deteriorated
> structures of compassion breaking down
> neighborhoods slowly rotting
> the poor despairing    unrest
> forever present in the land
>
> . . . . . . . .
>
> My brother's action helped me realize
> from the beginning    of our republic
> good men had said no
> acted outside the law
> when conditions so demanded
> And if a man did this
> time might vindicate him    show his act to be lawful
> a gift to society
> a gift to history
> and to the community.[12]

This is, to be sure, talking about conditions of distress which are not "normal." In the best of times restraint is admirable. Structures can assure freedom and provide the conditions for maximizing it. But when the support of them is a tacit support of oppression, the Christian is free to suspend his obligation to the orders of men. The opening up of our corporate life to new possibilities for freedom and fulfillment transcends in importance the virtues of orderly change. Those whose freedom is received from the promises of God may have to abort their commitments to the structures and laws of society in the creation of a more humane existence for all men.

The cynicism engendered by the seemingly insoluble quality of the social problems in our times has been sustained for many by the inability of our faith to cope with it. A version of Christianity that has been almost exclusively implemented in the realm of personal intimacy and private ethics cannot provide a base from which to support change in the social order. It should not have been surprising that most Protestants were shocked when an agency of the United Presbyterian Church gave financial support to the legal defense of Angela Davis. Aside from whether or not this was a legitimate use of funds, few churchmen had any grasp of the theological terms upon which that action might be taken. One cannot move from an understanding of a personal God related to our private hang-ups to a political act by the church. A privatized faith is no match for a political existence. However tempting and rewarding it may be for theology to be existential and relate to the personal struggles of men, it will in effect be an abstraction until the critical resources of faith are opened toward the social order. The exodus and the crucifixion were, after all, political events. The promises of God intersect the sociopolitical realities of the day. The task of theology now is to reset the tension between those promises and realities, thus opening up the recognition that the practice of hope is a public as well as personal event.

# II

# THE CREATURE
# WHO HOPES

The assumption of the first chapter was that man's capacity for
the future is not so much at the mercy of his personal crises as
of his institutional confinements. The most emotive and
threatening words are not anxiety, despair, and meaninglessness, but Attica, Kent State, and Cambodia. The "existing disorder" is more in the midst of us than within us. What is
required is a working out of the Christian faith with man's sociopolitical existence in view. But to wean Christianity from its
unwholesome alliance with the private does not preclude dealing with the nature of man. What gives rise to cynicism may
well be the tight environment in which he lives. But how does
this relate to an understanding of man as the creature who en-
dures this environment? What is it about man that protrudes
in the face of the forces of futurelessness?

## The Disposition to Hope

Any understanding of man makes an initial assumption concerning the level on which he will be interpreted. The exposure
of man's essential qualities and the identification of his distinctive form of functioning in the world processes occurs, for the
Biblical faith, on the historical plane. His sphere is not primarily physical or emotional, though it embraces both. Basically,
"man is a historical being. He is not born in the world of
things, persons, and time as a finished product. . . . He be-

comes what he is through the history of his relations with his environment. . . . He comes into being *with* the world. . . . Man changes. . . . Man responds. . . . And when he responds the world becomes different. It becomes historical." [13] History is his realm and the scene of his responses to nature in himself and about him. Certainly dimensions of man's existence can be appropriated through an examination of the stimuli exerted upon him, the chemical alterations within him, or such aggressive propensities as may be expressed in his social behavior. Each in its own way may be operative, but neither singularly or together do they provide the key to his nature.

What is it then that man on the canvas of history does distinctively and decisively? In the words of Ernst Bloch, he is "the creature who hopes." That does not mean man is a passive agent to whom a new future is given or that in the present he invents the future. It does mean that man has the capacity to see and reach beyond any present set of circumstances. His existence can explode toward the future. What is most authentic about man is the disposition to hope, to live from the future rather than in terms of the past and present. In hoping, man reaches beyond every apparent limit with anticipation, inquiry, and vision. He can set himself toward what is new and unknown rather than what is old and comfortable. Hope is not the calculation of a new future based on extrapolations from present data; it is a confidence that the unpredictable will happen. The most fundamental consciousness in man is a passionate longing for what is "not yet." When man is truly in possession of his existence, he experiences the process of hoping as a militant aspiration for something new in the future.

One of the characteristics of the moment is the steady cry and search for something which is radically new. Fascination with a new future animates the aspiration of Afro-Americans, mobilizes the dreams of a student generation, and creates the preoccupation of politicians with "the quality of life." Daydreams have been replaced by bold visions, reminiscing by anticipation, and despair by the courage to act. The protruding sensibility is expectancy. Such heroes as stalk our sagas and inhabit our history manifest a vigorous yearning for a new day. While poets and playwrights are said to form the images of the age to come, it may be said that in a time of cultural and social crisis a student generation mirrors what is coming of age. There one witnesses an astonishing willingness to anticipate a "new heaven and a new earth," to deny prediction in favor of vision, and to act as if the impossible was the only task worth assuming. Their counterculture engages in rhetoric, creates symbols, and participates in rituals which refuse to foreclose on any possibility for the future. In a time when one might indulge oneself in cynicism, there emerges a phenomenon which is zestful and joyful in the determination to hope.

But hope must be distinguished from optimism. Optimism is a sensibility marked by a belief that the future will be a marked improvement over the present. It is the feeling that things can and will get better; its scant Biblical warrant adheres in the mustard seed image associated with the Kingdom of God. The essential quality of optimism is a euphoric confidence in the inevitability of progress. It exists on the other side of alienation, tragedy, and existentialism. As such it canonizes progress. The flaws in its armor are at least twofold, and they mark it off from militant hope. Optimism rests on the confidence that reason can pierce through the future and rob it of mystery. By contrast, "the man who hopes is not making the irritating claim to know more about the future than others. Christian eschatology therefore is not an ideology of the future. It values precisely the poverty of its knowledge about the future." [14] Hope is aggressive in its expectancy but does not presume to grasp precisely what it expects. The model is evident in Heb. 11:8: "By faith Abraham obeyed the call to go out to a land destined for himself and his heirs and left home not knowing where he was to go." The mystery of the future and the forms of fulfillment contained in promises can be trusted but not predicted or penetrated. Optimism and hope come from different directions. The former sees the future developing in the present and therefore can risk predictions; the latter sees the future intruding into the present and therefore hopes all the more.

Secondly, optimism does not take serious account of human sin or the corruption in man's endeavors. It bypasses the dark side of existence in favor of perfectability. H. Richard Niebuhr has depicted the way in which optimism has twisted the Christian message of the Kingdom: "A God without wrath brought men without sin into a kingdom without judgment through the ministrations of a Christ without a cross." But militant hope sets itself against the sin of man from the perspective of the future; it does not set it aside. And the account hope takes of sin reveals the radical quality of its hoping. Hope has no illusions about the nature of man. It embraces finitude but all the more the future. In optimism "men have ceased to believe in the devil and no longer have an eye for the cashiered side of transcendence." [15] Hope is based on a real future emerging not in ignorance of "the devil" but against his most fiendish labors.

When man hopes, he is open to the future; existence is experienced as possibility. But to have a future is threatening. One has to be open to possibilities he cannot control; indeed, the possibilities of a real future by their nature escape control. Militant hope is an act of exposure to the future, which is not only unpredictable but demanding. Life is set in tension between promises, the scope of which cannot be measured, and present conditions, the limitations of which are unacceptable. In response, man escapes into forms of stasis that by forestalling the future preserve the present in some manageable form. Sin, the perversion of human existence, is then the attempt to reset the tension at a lower frequency or banish it. In the process of unlearning hope, man gets out from under responsibility.

In the mythical Garden of Eden, Adam and Eve were given provision for their needs and the promise of fulfillment in their administration of creation. But mystery was a boundary; they were forbidden to eat the fruit. Adam and Eve overstepped the boundary and ate the forbidden fruit. Yet the origin of sin is not initially in the defiance but in the abdication of responsibility. "Eve shares with Adam the assignment of exercising

mastery over all the creatures of the field. Her 'original' mis-
deed was not eating the forbidden fruit at all. Before she
reached for the fruit, she had already surrendered her position
of power and responsibility over one of the animals, the serpent, and let it tell her what to do." [16] Sin is reneging on the
future in one form or another. Eve spent her destiny by giving
it away; the dispersal of responsibility is the beginning of the
end of hope. For in hoping man holds himself to the future as
it interacts with the present. He cannot say, "The serpent be-
guiled me" (Gen. 3:13), for that means man is no longer open
to the future. He forfeits his humanity when his loyalty to the
future is compromised by some alliance in the present. He
ceases to hope militantly; the future becomes closed. And
when man no longer hopes, he has aborted freedom, thus ac-
cepting the present conditions as those which will establish the
future. In "leaving it to the snake," man indicates that he is no
longer expecting something really new; he has settled for a limited horizon of possibilities. He has avoided the tensions created
by the future for the more tolerable conditions he can manage
in the present. Hope is not militant but domesticated.

## The Grounds of Hope

To have affirmed hope as the essential quality of human existence is not to have identified an insatiable instinct or a self-
sustaining process in man. Man hopes in relation to something.
Hope banks on a reality that is not itself but that calls it into
force. Man's hoping has a context. But what is it that activates
this capacity for the future? What is it that gives man the critical distance from his present pain and enables him to act
against it in the hope of a better future? There would seem to
be two main lines of argument. One is what Rubem Alves calls
"political humanism." Hope is activated by hopelessness; in
the experience of the contradiction of his humanity man lashes
back with a negation of the negative. Those who suffer futurelessness respond by denying the present. In fact, it is only "the

slaves, the wretched of the earth, the outcasts and marginals
. . . who can have the vision and passion for and are able to
understand the language of hope, freedom, and liberation." [17]
Hope happens because of the hopelessness in which man finds
himself. Only those fully abused in the present can forcefully
hope for a new future. Those who have no future rebel against
futurelessness, their rebellion taking the form of hope. Only
they have nothing to lose by risking everything. Hope is born
in despair, not confidence. "Political humanism" overlaps with
the Biblical understanding of hope in the recognition that only
the futureless are likely to do anything about their condition.
The wealthy and powerful are seldom if ever the agents of God's
promised future. Their stake in the present is too high. Jesus
did not hold high prospects for the rich entering the coming
Kingdom; they were too embedded in the kingdom of the now.
Comfort is not a likely source of discontent! Yet for all the
truth in that, the confidence that the oppressed will rise up
against their condition and aspire durably to a new future is
unwarranted. Accommodation can as readily be born of despair.
Those without a hope can make peace with that condition. It
is not necessarily the case that those who suffer will become
those who protest. Liberating aspiration can be domesticated
with a few cheap concessions until one is resting the prospects
of freedom on a "happy slave." Hopelessness is not sufficient
ground for activating hope in any permanent form.

The alternative to grounding hope in man's capacity for self-
transcendence and his aversion to present conditions is to see
the process of hope sustained by God. Man's propensity to
hope is given durability by God's identification with man in his
struggle against the present. God himself experiences the resistance of the old order of futurelessness and suffers under and
against it. In a subsequent chapter we will consider the nature
and impact of God's suffering. Here we can only affirm that the
suffering of God is the ground of hope. Experiencing the violence done to our lives as done to him, he himself engages the
forces of futurelessness and creates the possibility of hoping.
Only a suffering God can maintain hope for something new.

THE CREATURE WHO HOPES                39

The nature of God's activity in the world is to negate the phenomena that deny man's being and his possibilities. Even
when man chooses the security of futurelessness and makes his
peace with the present, God suffers in loneliness. The context
of hope, then, is not merely man's experience of hopelessness;
that can indeed yield the critical distance that incites protest.
But the durability of hope is grounded in an ultimate determination to open the future. One can invert the formula and
affirm that when man hopes durably and with sustained militancy, it is an experience of God suffering alongside him. "The
experience of reaching out beyond every limit in the present toward a fuller freedom of life is the form under which modern
man can experience the transcendence of God today. . . . If
God is pictured as the liberator of mankind, luring men beyond
every kind of bondage under the existing set of facts, there is
psychologically no longer any need to opt for atheism for the
sake of freedom. God is the power who supports man in the
struggle for freedom. He is the sustaining ground of hope for
liberation." [18]

The implication in what has been said is that there is a
relationship between hope and memory. The man who hopes
passionately longs for something new in the future because he
remembers promises which have been honored in the past and
which yield intimations of the coming future. This is not to
imply a recycling of the acts of God; the myths of eternal re-
turn are the enemies of hope. To see the new as a recurrence of
the old is a virulent form of expectancy. The ways of God in
the world are not like the late-late movies, which are reruns:
some things may have been omitted but nothing new has been
added. In the Biblical faith, hope is defined not by what has
been but by what will be. This not only sets the viability of
hoping but suggests the qualities for which one may indeed
hope. The coming future is not altogether unknown; while remaining unpredictable and startlingly new, it has yielded
glimpses that are often only recognized in retrospect. While the
past is never more than provisional, it contains announcements
of what is forthcoming. Thus one can say that "hope exists in

the mode of memory and memory in the mode of hope." [19] In the promissory history of Biblical faith, man hopes because he remembers, and he remembers because he hopes. Memory is the internal form of hope and hope the actualization of memory. Hope has a history that is the basis of confidence in the coming future.

Hope overcomes cynicism by pointing to the honor of God. God mediates in history a consciousness of anticipation. The community of faith remembers how God as the power of the future called Abraham to live by the promise that if he left the security of his homeland, he would be an instrument in the creation of a great nation. This was the inauguration of a consciousness that one could break with the present sources of security and endure the anxiety of the unknown. The quality of "hoping against hope" is remembered in the person of Moses. What could have been more hopeless than the representative of slaves standing before the Pharaoh and demanding liberation? But in the strength of promises, Moses did just that; and when the heart of Pharaoh stiffened, he led the Israelites out of Egypt in the confidence God would be ahead of them. Moses commanded no army; perhaps they didn't even have a pocket knife among them! But he practiced hope. The faith of the New Testament community is written against this background. Jesus' message of the coming Kingdom, legitimated by the cross and resurrection, is the matrix from which Christians live forward toward a new future. We should not be entirely self-conscious when Ernst Bloch testifies that "the total expansion of hope that we find in humanism came into the world only in one form—that of the Bible." [20] The possibility of militant hope is sustained by the memory of those who, against the realistic prospect of the present, trusted the promises of something new in the future and were not deceived. Hope has a history which makes hoping legitimate. The context of hope is God's faithfulness to his promises in suffering alongside man in history on behalf of another future. To abide in hope is to fix oneself in history, both remembering and anticipating God as the power of the future.

### Loyalty to Hope

Man lives in an interval of tension, between the time of the issuance of God's promises and their fulfillment. The authenticity of his existence between the times is resolved in terms of his "loyalty to hope." Paradoxical as it may sound, while man cannot initiate the coming of the future, he is obligated to do something about hope. It is not the prerogative of man to invent the future, nor will its coming be a result of his achievement. The future comes to man; it is not brought on by him. Yet the future does not just happen! Hope demands planning and initiatives that are responsive to the expectancy; loyalty to hope takes some present form in anticipation of the future. It requires imagining an unimaginable future and, in the feeble ways at our disposal, doing something about it. Anticipation of the future sets one to the task of discerning the forms in which hope can be practiced. In this sense Christian hope is not blind optimism that waits passively for the future. The militancy of hope is not emotional rage but a determination to be loyal to the promises of God in the time and place in which we find ourselves. Hope involves the responsibility "to represent Christian freedom in the realm of political reason and in the public conflicts of our society." [21] Clearly, giving the future full play in human existence has consequences that threaten present formulations of responsibility.

When man allows his existence to be fleshed out by militant hope, his responsiveness to the promises sets him at odds with the structures of the present. Having existence in terms of hope, he runs against the formulations of hopelessness in society. The paradigm for that is Jesus of Nazareth; he lived a life of contradiction, not accommodation. William Stringfellow contends that the most faithful and suggestive image we can apply to him is that of criminal. From the perspective of the state and the religious authorities of the day he was "not a mere non-conformist, not just a protester, more than a militant, not only a dissident, not simply a dissenter, but a criminal." [22] The charge was "perverting [the] nation" and "forbidding . . . tribute" to the state (Luke 23:3).

Insofar as Jesus was seditious and subversive on the world's terms, he was a more reprehensible criminal than Barabbas. He differed from Barabbas in that his challenge to the system was based on the power of the future and therefore constituted a permanent threat and revolt. It was not a provisional revolt against this and that but radical contradiction of authority. The practice of hope set him at odds with embodiments of hopelessness; his commitment to the future set him against all the forms of futurelessness. And the world cannot abide that degree of threat. It has to preserve the arrangements of the now and crucify any forms of aspiration for the new. Jesus was a criminal, beneath all the particular charges, because hope held full sway. He repudiated the structures of death in the present, structures which sustained futurelessness. One thing has to be said about the political and ecclesiastical authorities: they knew exactly what was "coming down" in Jesus of Nazareth. He was not falsely accused, neither was he denied due process. In the full measure of the Roman legal tradition, he was guilty.

The militant hope embodied in the life and death and resurrection of Jesus reset priorities. The establishment of the day said, "Caesar is king; worship and obey him." But the gospel is: "There is another king, Jesus." Hope does awful things to the world—on the world's terms. It denies those terms in affirmation of freedom for the future. It points men out toward the future and then back into the present with a militancy the world can only read as virulent. "Christ as King means Man no mere servant of the State or any other authority, no incapacitated victim of a damaged environment. Christ as King means Man free from bondage to ideologies and institutions, free from revolutionary causes as well, free from idolatry of Caesar and, not the least of it, free from religion that tries to disguise such slaveries as virtuous, free from all these and similar claims that really conceal only death—only the dehumanization of life —for men." [23] Hope frees a man to be a criminal on the world's terms. Not all criminals are Christians, perhaps not even many; but all Christians are suspect to the degree that they practice hope.

There is always an arbitrary element in naming faithful embodiments of the way of Jesus in one's own time. One may tend to sanctify his heroes; but the alternative is to deny the presence of God in one's own day by timidity. Two men seem to stand as embodiments of militant hope and in the model of criminality. Dietrich Bonhoeffer is one. He had said that when Jesus calls a man, he calls him to come and die. Discipleship ultimately leads to the cross because the Christian is called against the world by the future. The form in which that call came to Bonhoeffer was the Nazi regime, which negated freedom. He chose to act against that evil by participation in a plot to assassinate Hitler. While not commending it as every Christian's duty, he understood it as his own. For the practice of hope in the world he died at the hands of worldly power.

Less dramatic but no less vivid is the life of Father Daniel Berrigan. In a number of ways he and his brother have chosen to act against a system which they see as the embodiment of death. On one occasion, while Berrigan was avoiding arrest for acting against the law, he appeared in a church in the Germantown section of Philadelphia and preached on the text from Hebrews that begins, "Now faith is the assurance of things hoped for, the conviction of things not seen" (Heb. 11:1). Speaking then of how they chose to embody hope in their own lives, Berrigan said: "We have chosen to be powerless criminals in a time of criminal power. We have chosen to be branded as peace criminals by war criminals." Believing that the law is being used to break the law of our humanity, Berrigan feels free to break the law of the nation and finally to assume the consequences. Hope affirms that the world can be changed, that reality is not fixed; in the practice of hope a man is judged to be seditious.

## The Limits of Hope

Hope has no earthbound limits; the man of hope suffers under and against the present structures. This drives him to answer the question, how militant dare hope be? What about violence? Hope by its fixation on the future disrupts the normal course of events. But how much disruption is legitimate? Some have resolved the problem by defining violence as at times necessary but never legitimate for the Christian. Circumstances may force a responsible person into a position where he has to suspend nonviolence, but he does this in the knowledge that he is acting outside the norms of faith. Surely that constitutes an avoidance of the issue. And ironically it yields a broad response with a narrow grasp of the dimensions of violence. It does not attend to the question of whose the violence is and what forms it takes.

Rubem Alves enhances understanding considerably when he points out that two different answers to the question, "What is violence?" can be given. "From the point of view of the man who is afraid of the future and who, therefore, has built structures to defend himself against it, violence is everything that disturbs or threatens the world his fear has built." [24] Whenever factors come into play which portend change, project the new in society, and oppose the structures which assure him of security, violence is in evidence. Such power as a man may exercise in supporting order is not violence but a legitimate form of self-preservation. Thus wars of national self-interest are perceived as legitimate and noble acts in defense of freedom, while domestically the aspiration to freedom of the oppressed is a defiance if force comes into play. Now, "from the point of view of the man who is free for the future, violence is . . . whatever denies him a future, whatever aborts his project to create a new tomorrow. . . . Violence is the power of defuturization, which strives to close man's consciousness to the future and the future to man's consciousness." [25] Then violence is the master on the slaves' backs, and it is legitimate for the slave to use whatever means necessary to get free of the master. From the perspective of the third world, colonialism is violence; it denies the colonialized the possibility of a totally new future. We cannot, then, recognize violence by disruption or identify it with the spilling of blood. The determination of what is violence pivots on where a man stands—in the present or on behalf of the future. From the vantage point of hope, violence is anything that supports, institutes, or perpetuates futurelessness. From the vantage point of the system and those committed to its continuance, violence is anything that threatens the smooth functioning of society. To this extent, the question of violence is a relative one. Once one has landed here, the issue becomes: whose violence shall I support? The assumption, then, is that violence in fact exists. Granted the way in which the world is given to us, the choice for the Christian is not violence versus nonviolence but which form of violence he will support. He may have to make a judgment between the violence embedded in the system and the violence required to overthrow it. It is meaningless, then, to come out for or against violence; what goes to the heart of the issue is the questions raised about the utilization of force. A determination has to be made at the outset concerning the degree of futurelessness sustained in the system. If it totally suffocates human freedom, the Christian is obligated to use the power necessary to release man from bondage.

On the other hand, the counterpower may be leveled at making the system more flexible so that the exercise of freedom is possible within it. Certainly one must ask whether bringing the old forms of dominance to a stop will in fact give birth to liberating conditions. Frantz Fanon in the context of Africa has noted that the purge of colonial powers does not relieve the plight of the oppressed if an indigenous elite are left in power. The negation of the negative must indeed be in behalf of a better future! Then the means of power brought into force must be proportionate to the humane goals of the opposition. Can the new society indeed control the violence unleashed in overthrowing the old one? One ought also to calculate the prospects of transformation; in the utilization of force. Can one project the likelihood of "success"? Great delicacy is involved in combining aspiration with the prospects of accomplishment.

The militancy of hope has no boundaries save those which God as the power of the future imposes in the present. Violence is an issue subordinate to that of the just use and misuse of power. The expectation of something new always meets resistance; it comes up against powers erected to preserve the old orders and prevent the incursion of the new. The forces of liberation then become subversive powers which seek to bring a halt to the forms of bondage. In history the aspiration to freedom and the processes of death inevitably conflict; the power of the future and the constraint of the present confront one another. Thus, "the man who . . . hopes will never be able to reconcile himself with the laws and constraints of this earth. . . . Hope finds in Christ not only a consolation in suffering, but also the protest of the divine promises against suffering. . . . Faith takes up this contradiction and thus becomes itself a contradiction to the world of death. That is why faith, whenever it develops into hope, causes not rest but unrest, not patience but impatience. It does not calm the unquiet heart, but is itself this unquiet heart in man." [26] To live for and from the future is to refuse to endure reality as it is, and in suffering under and against it, to be a free man who is committed to making room for the creation of the new.

By way of summary, our experience of the sociopolitical realities of our lives may drive us in the direction of cynicism about the prospects of the future. But there is in the nature of man a disposition to hope; he is the creature who can live toward the possibilities of the future at the very moment when the actualities of the present are most gruesome. The durability of that process, however, is a function of God's identification with man's struggle for an open future and his suffering with us against the forces of futurelessness. When a man holds himself to hope in the promises of God, he may indeed become a criminal in the world's terms. Those who suspend loyalty to the present are vulnerable to the charge of treason. And they often find themselves in the position of utilizing violence, not because they believe in it, but because the alternatives are both violent. By its nature, hope is a militant act; inevitably it disrupts the present.

# III

# THE POWER OF THE FUTURE

The reality of God does not inevitably protrude into our consciousness or thought processes. Perhaps it once did. But one of the meanings of the death of God movement is that we can no longer take for granted the question of God. The issue goes beyond a threat to the assumption of an absolute and to categories of thought that emerge from that premise. The problem is that the transcendent intrudes as an afterthought; even among the faithful it is often affirmed self-consciously and without confidence. The reality of God is now something we have to work toward rather than work from. The priority for theologians, then, is not to identify the most authentic word to be said about God, but to identify the form in which the question of God can be raised. By way of analogy, the issue is not how to play chess but how to get on the chessboard.

How *does* the question of God get raised in our day? An initial clue comes in the recognition that man's understanding of himself and his understanding of God are intrinsically related. The picture held of existence is continuous with the picture which emerges of an Ultimate. This is not to contend that the Ultimate is something human taken to the nth degree. But it is to affirm that man must look to himself to discern how he can gain access to the reality of God. He will not find within himself any substantive data on the nature of God but he will find what it is in his own experience that points toward that reality. In the previous chapter we represented man as the creature who hopes. The controlling experience he has of himself is of a being who is in the process of becoming and who anticipates fulfillment from the future. While aware of what is, he clings to what will be. His most authentic sense of himself is in leaning forward. It is this picture of existence which leads Carl Braaten to ask, "Might it not be that eschatology is the key to the recovery of a doctrine of God 'after the death of God?' " [27] The question of the future can raise the question of God. And it focuses the possibility of interpreting God as the power of the future.

## The Eschatological Framework

But the readiness of man in this age for a new future is not what legitimates doing theology in an eschatological key. Certainly it is true that disruptions and aspirations in our culture shape the modes of religious experience. Social change dislodges trusted formulations and provides the occasion for a new mode in the formation of faith. That a theology should avail itself of a mood and a sensibility is not surprising; at best it always correlates an understanding of the Biblical message with the dominant quality of experience in an age. The issue of legitimacy, however, is not resolved by the criteria of contemporaneity; it is resolved within the terms set forth by the Biblical faith. Futurity is fundamental to the Christian message; hope is a core category for faith. The early Christians set their message in an eschatological framework when they proclaimed the coming rule of God as the fulfillment of man's hope. While the culture may activate the eschatological dimension of Christianity, the authenticity of operating in that perspective is confirmed on other terms.

There is nothing new about an emphasis upon eschatology. While there have been times in which aspects of it could be referred to as the "Cinderella of Credal doctrines," [28] its genuineness as a whole is difficult to dispute. No less a theologian than Karl Barth affirms that in the measure that our understanding of the faith is controlled by Christ it is pervasively eschatological. Yet to have agreed upon that does not specify what eschatology itself means. It may be helpful at this point to make some distinctions according to "brand names."

One of the most obvious, "imminent eschatology," is formed in the consciousness that the end is very near. The earliest Christians were possessed by the conviction that they were living in the last days: "Truly, I say to you, there are some standing here who will not taste death before they see the kingdom of God come with power" (Mark 9:1). Almost two thousand years later there are those who still talk as if Jesus' coming will be in their lifetimes. But the usual fate of "imminent eschatology" is to postpone the end indefinitely. Jesus, then, is no longer related to as a coming Lord but as a source of mighty spiritual forces in the present. The intensification of present experience under the impact of an expected end is liquidated; hope becomes an attitude rather than a priority in the logic of faith.

By contrast, "realized eschatology" relegates the essential qualities of fulfillment to the past. The decisive event for the future has already happened and the present is a time of working out the consequences. The future is in effect, rather than anticipated. The analogy is often used of a war in which at one point a decisive battle is won that determines the outcome, while skirmishes remain to be fought. Specifically, a decisive victory was effected in Jesus of Nazareth and from that point forward Christians have conceived of themselves as living in a new age. Their task is to implement that victory in their time. But in the twentieth century there is something which rings hollow in the claim that fulfillment was in the first century and we have been in the process of actualizing it ever since. It is tempting to protest that the new age that has been realized did not amount to much.

"Demythologized eschatology" emerges as an attempt to give substance to the present. Its existential emphasis virtually eliminates the future dimension. Drawing heavily upon the Fourth Gospel, yet supported by Paul, those who hold this view understand the future event not as something which will happen or has happened but as something which can happen in any given moment. While it cannot be denied that certain events in the life of Christ did occur, they are to be understood as recurring in the life of the Christian. In the face of his own death, each man has occasion to participate in the death and resurrection of Christ, and therefore in freedom for his possibilities. Aside from the tendency of this posture to be very individual and to forfeit the corporate character of existence, it is defuturizing. There is no end time and no end event. The future refers to no more than the next moment in which the Christian appropriates for himself the truth of faith.

A commitment to preserve the reality of the future is represented in "futuristic eschatology." It does not postpone the future indefinitely, it does not count the future as realized and now in the process of actualization, nor does it dehistoricize the future by making it a present occurrence. The future is not perceived as the present running ahead of itself; neither is it an expansion of the past. The future gives the present and past their reality. The vision of reality is that it is really ahead of us; the future is not a consequence of the past and the present but a determinant of both. What will be affects what is and what has been. The future is seen as that which acts upon the moments in which we find ourselves and gives them their reality. It is the future that brings things together now and sets their nature. What is radical in this understanding of eschatology is not only its affirmation of a real future and the future as reality but its contention that eschatology is the key in which Christianity must be set. It is not a part of Christian doctrine but the mode in which it authentically exists. Christianity is eschatology: it centers on the future.

When we embrace Braaten's claim that eschatology is the key in which the doctrine of God ought to be set after the death of God, it is "futuristic eschatology" we have in mind. The Christian faith is centered in anticipations of a real future that preempts both fantasy and cynicism. That future is not a development of latent forces in history or the production of men with a healthy respect for divinity. The Christian is hooked on a future which "is to come in a marvelous way from God himself. . . ." [29] If we are to affirm God in the face of our own disposition to hope, we will need to develop an understanding of him in futuristic categories. We need concepts and images that represent him as One who is ahead of us.

Yet our theological instincts tend to move in the other direction; our understanding of transcendence is formed by an extrapolation from the past. We proceed from what God has done to what he will do. And that has a distinct legitimacy. The Judeo-Christian tradition understands God as Liberator through his record of liberating activity. His identity is opened to us by events in our history that have had that quality to them. The exodus is certainly central in establishing God as the deliverer of the people of Israel. What the Israelites knew about God was formed initially in the experience of being brought out of bondage. When the vision of God tarried, priests and prophets in word, deed, and ritual rehearsed that drama and reactivated the image of God as Liberator. Through the ministry, death, and resurrection of Jesus, the early Christian community formed a picture of God as Savior. He was the One who overcame death and opened the future to new life. And that understanding of living in a new age is reactivated in the Christian community through its worship and its sacraments. Around the foci of exodus and Jesus, Christians have been informed by an understanding of God as Liberator; he works to set men free of their bondages and death. It is tempting to witness that and say, "Now, the future is more of the same." Then what is ahead is a recycling of what has gone before. But that is to assume that God is incapable of doing something new. The Christian looks back through the community of faith not in order to extrapolate but in order to anticipate. The past of faith has a futurizing effect. It teaches him to look ahead and respond to the pull of the future. From the past he learns to anticipate surprises; he does not learn what these surprises will be.

## Ernst Bloch

Some will note that one can be eschatological without being theological, concentrate upon a coming future without the vision of a God who brings it into being. Without embarrassment it must be conceded that theologians have no monopoly on the futurist perspective. Indeed, it could be argued that they have ignored this category of thought. Perhaps it will be illuminating to consider briefly an eschatological framework without a theistic dimension. Ernst Bloch provides a particularly apt illustration. This atheistic Marxist presents a philosophy which correlates human aspiration for the new with an affirmation of the position of reality in the future. As such he holds a striking fascination for theologians. Yet for all the affinities, he affirms the future without a transcendent, and it is this which is of interest here.

Ernst Bloch's vision of reality is not that it exists but that it is becoming. For him the future is the pivotal category and hope is its derivative sensibility. The essence of a thing is not what it is but what it will be. Both human existence and nature are a process moving toward fulfillment. "Not-yetness" is the quality of everything. "It is only the horizon of the future . . . which gives to reality its real dimension." [30] While the future is decided in the present, its possibilities are not latent potentialities but rather are the power of the future drawing the present to fulfillment. Human decision coupled with militant hope are functions of the action of the future upon the incomplete quality of man and nature. The end creates the beginning. Yet for Bloch the future is a direction, not a destination; it is not something at which one arrives but something toward which one always moves. The future is leverage; it effects newness in the present. And hope is the subjective response to this vision of reality. For Bloch it is this which gives rise to religion. Where there is hope, there is religion; and where there is religion, there is hope. "According to Bloch, the longing that gives rise to religion, the desire of oppressed creation for joy, for happiness, and for hope, has its roots in that dichotomy in man which is so pregnant with religion—the dichotomy between his present appearance and his nonpresent essence." [31] In this context God is not a reality in and of himself but a utopian symbol expressing what man is to be. God stands for undiscovered future humanity. Bloch is an atheist; he denies the existence of God because he thinks that would mean the future is not really open and is already determined. But still it is by gods that men express their movement toward a longed-for future.

Why ought theology not to yield to a philosophy of hope? Obviously that would enhance its credibility in certain quarters. Aside from the fact that theology would be abdicating responsibility, there are some obstacles. Moltmann identifies, and then dismisses, one that on the surface would be persuasive. It might be argued that the experience of the absurd cuts the ground out from under the disposition to hope. Those events whose irrationality depletes our expectations tend to contradict the openness of the future. The futility that they engender short-circuits hope. But Christian eschatology would be equally vulnerable before that argument. The differences between theology of hope and philosophy of hope break at other points. Therefore, it is more productive to concentrate upon identifying those features of Christian hope which are preempted by Bloch's philosophy. The problem centers on his reduction of God to a symbol gathering up the longed-for future, the transcendent deity over against the "not-yetness" of man and the world. This inevitably raises the question, "What keeps man alive, keeps him moving, hoping, and pressing forward?" [32] What is it that prevents hope from degenerating into an attitude? What is it that precipitates the anticipating consciousness and sustains militant hope? Bloch's defense is in terms of a materialist foundation. The basis of hope is finally in matter's quality of longing for form, matter's inherent "forwardness." But what is the hope behind that hoping? The answer must be hope. Hope is built on hoping, which cannot finally sustain it. Now what is significant is that in this process Bloch has undercut the radicality of his professed eschatology. By going back to matter as possessing the quality of longing for the future, he does not in fact begin at the end. Without a transcendent who is the power of the future, he works to the future rather than from it. The ground of the future is not in the future but in matter. The latency of matter is incompatible with a radically futuristic perspective. "Without the transcendence of God, the future's transcendence is mired in the matter of creation. The result of Bloch's demythologizing of God, oddly, is his remythologizing of nature, transferring to nature what belongs to God. . . . Christian hope is based on the power of God's future, not on the inner possibilities of matter." [33]

The philosophy of hope, as expressed through its most persuasive advocate, is not a substitute for a theology of hope. Bloch is not "all wrong," but in the last resort his understanding of hope collapses against itself. There is nothing finally from the future to support it. What is called for in an understanding of man as a "hope-er" is an affirmation of One whose own reality is in the future and brings us into being through the present.

### God and the Future

Returning to our premise that the question of the future can raise the question of God, we need to identify how the reality of God connects with the disposition of man to hope. What has God to do with the future? The response shared within the perspective of the theology of hope is that God's reality is in the future; his existence is future tense. He is experienced as One ahead of us opening up our possibilities in the present. In a sense, we do not meet God as an eternal now but as an eternal then. His way of being with us is as One who calls us forth from the future. That is set before us with particular vividness through the experience of Moses while tending his father-in-law's sheep. Drawn to the phenomenon of a burning bush that was not consumed, he was addressed by the God of his fathers: "I have seen the affliction of my people who are in Egypt. . . . I know their sufferings, and I have come down to deliver them out of the hand of the Egyptians" (Ex. 3:7-8). Not a bad offer. But Moses anticipated that his people would want to know the source of this promise; they were remarkably unaware of God. Asked Moses, "If I come to the people of Israel and say to them, 'The God of your fathers has sent me to you,' and they ask me, 'What is his name?' what shall I say to them?" (Ex. 3:13.) For a Hebrew, if one knew a person's name, one was taken into his identity and could assume a confident relationship. God instructs Moses to give the Israelites this word, "I will be what I will be," or, "I cause to be what I cause to be." He promised to be known to them in the events to come; he identified himself as the One who would be ahead of them, leading them forward. In the strength of that promise Moses challenged Pharaoh; Moses and his people walked away from their bondage.

God is the giver of the future. We experience him not as One who is fully actualized and with us in all his splendor but as One who is himself coming into his fullness. He confronts us in his becoming and gathers us up into the process of coming to be. Futurity is the distinctive quality of God's own being and his insertion into our existence is in the form of the power of the future. It is his futurity which yields man a legitimate future. The pervasive experience for man is of the loss of a future. He is restricted and restrained by a present determined by the past; his notion of the future is that it is void of surprises. But God as the power of the future sets a new priority. The present is not a function of what has been but of what will be. The determinant of existence is the future. The vision of reality is constructed from what is becoming. What the encounter of God with Moses did was to subordinate the past and present to the future. In the measure that the Israelites accepted their present state and calculated their chances of its changing, they had no future except as a repetition of their recent history. But they were given a new horizon, the promise of a new future. And that neutralized their immersion in what was. Through the power of the future they negated the present. Their prospects were formed in the recognition that there was One who could make available to them a totally new future. We may understand God, then, as "ahead of us in the horizons of the future opened to us in his promises." [34] He is the God of a coming world, yet present in such a way as to form this world in the light of the future.

This understanding of God invites comparison with process theology, which affirms development in the reality of God with a particular emphasis upon human input into his becoming. There is a substantial overlap, in that both futuristic eschatology and process theology deny the existence of God as an absolute who is now what he always has been and always will be. Both affirm time in the essence of God in opposition to those who affirm his eternity as timelessness. The nature of God is that he is coming into his being and therefore into his existence. But there is a point at which the similarity ends abruptly. Process theology claims that the message of the Kingdom of God implies that there is development in the Godhead in response to the human condition; God's becoming moves toward the future from a present that in a limited sense defines the future of God. Futuristic eschatology lays stress upon the coming of God from his future, affecting man's present and past. God is not being created along the way; man and the world are. God as the coming One is capable of doing what we might not expect, something truly new; but "what turns out to be true in the future will then be evident as having been true all along." [35] God's coming into his being is, in a sense, according to plan and therefore not open to redefinition in the process.

To understand God as coming into his existence, rather than having already arrived, is an important wedge into the contemporary consciousness, which cannot cope meaningfully with absolutes. Paul van Buren may overstate the case when he says that the assumption of an absolute is no longer operational. That has the disadvantage of being itself a rather absolute statement; but more importantly, it obscures the hidden absolutes functioning in many scientific and political systems. Yet it is true that the absolute as an operative image in our experience and thinking has receded, and our ways of responding and conceptualizing reflect more directly the radical contingency of all that is. The sensibility of the age is not only future-oriented, but as a result is informed by a vision of reality full of possibility. Things are not set; and this permeates all realms of human experience. "Man no longer experiences nature as a fixed and completed reality. Modern science and technology have made nature the site for constructing the human world. We no longer view the structure of society as given by nature or by God, but we know that because they are made by man they can be changed by man. People used to feel themselves personally responsible to these structures; today they feel themselves communally responsible for these structures. They are no longer authoritarian structures, but functional forms of corporate existence." [36] The dominant vision of reality in the contemporary consciousness is that things are on the way to what they are going to be and our decisions make a difference. The terms are not wholly set in advance; change and transformation define the immediate horizon upon which one operates.

While this phenomenon has often had a shattering impact, it is more importantly an opportunity. In our time the question of God can arise with the question of the future. With faith's understanding of God as he who goes before us and defines the present in the power of his future, the connection with the contemporary understanding of reality and the prevailing sensibility of hope may not be inevitable but is at least susceptible to contact. This is not to obscure the difficulties in joining the hopes of men with the promises of God. But it is at the very least to affirm that when a person centers on the issue of hope for the future, he may be responsive to the affirmation of God as the power of the future. Contemporary man may not be eager for us to raise the question of God together with the question of the future; they do not inevitably reach for one another, as some might suggest. But the theologian with the secular aspirations in one hand and the Christian hopes in the other has compatible realities with which to begin the apologetic task.

## Jesus and the Future

It is important now that we explore the support that there is in the event of Jesus for understanding God as the power of the future. If futurity is the essential nature of God, then there must be some sense in which it is promised and present in Jesus of Nazareth. In Jesus' preaching of the Kingdom, God is identified as having futurity as his distinctive quality. "Jesus defined God for us in terms of the imminent future of his Kingdom. . . . He knew God in terms of the promises that had been given to Israel. He packed the promises and the hopes of Israel into his preaching of the Kingdom. . . . When Jesus said, 'Seek ye first the kingdom of God,' he fused the reality of God's Kingdom into his very being." [87] What is significant in his teaching is not only the temporal placing of God in the future, but the implicit recognition of a "not yet" quality in God himself. God is not only known in the form of promise and fulfillment; this very tension exists within his being. Promise and fulfillment are traditional devices for understanding the work of God in history, but here the claim is made that they suggest his nature. What God is to be is the same as the fulfillment promised in the coming Kingdom; promises are the form in which he is with us in the present. What this translates into for our understanding of God and history is that he is the power of the future. Hopes do not depend for their fulfillment upon the persistence of our hoping but upon the drive within God to bring to pass his promises. In the bringing of his Kingdom, God is bringing himself, and that raises the stakes radically above the possibilities anticipated on other terms. Clearly, then, in his message of the Kingdom, Jesus preached a God who was coming in his present reign with the fulfillment to which his promises pointed.

The confirmation of Jesus' teaching is in the resurrection: "through it God defined himself as the power of the future beyond the finality of death." [38] The resurrection event definitively opens up to us the future as God's mode of being and makes available to us a share in the promises of fulfillment. Beyond vindicating Jesus and his message, it is the resurrection that enables us to understand the radical openness of history to the future. There we understand God as "not yet" but also as the ultimate power of what will be. He who can break the chain of death in the resurrection of Jesus is in fact one in whom the promise of a new future has legitimacy and persuasiveness. Warrant for trust in God as the power of the future is present in God's response to the death of Jesus. With his message of the Kingdom we come up against the future as God's mode of being and the promise of the power of God to bring fulfillment: in the resurrection of Jesus we witness the capacity of God to make good on his promises and to initiate the liberating process in history. And it is the basis of all Christian hope.

Now we are not left in the dark concerning what the future will be like. "The proclamation of the Kingdom and its confirmation by the raising of Jesus from the dead are events of the past that in proleptic power are also the promise of the future." [39] Without ceasing to be ahead of us, the future has been in our midst. The future has entered into history and provided previews of the end. What is distinctive about futuristic eschatology is that it is obsessed with Jesus and the future. We have a fragmentary vision of reality, not knowing it fully as it will be but experiencing it in the process of becoming. In Jesus, man is given enough to go on, a foretaste that has "proleptic power." Man not only is given an understanding of the dimensions of love but is grasped from the future by its actualizing power; man not only has an image of the quality of grace overcoming sin but is drawn into its contagious power; man not only is granted a vision of righteousness revealing the perversity of the age but is caught up in its coming to be. All that it means to be human occurred in Jesus of Nazareth, yet becomes a process in history where in the power of God the present is energized by the future. Futuristic eschatology is not only directed by a vision of the future that has made its appearance in the present, but it is activated and sustained by its power as it reaches into the present. The hidden future has been announced and glimpsed, anticipated and incarnated, and thus influences the present by awakening hope.

But what is the relationship between the Christian idea of the future and the futurological tendencies operative in our world—moods and models existing alongside those of faith? To the degree that futuristic eschatology is concerned with Jesus and the future, it is tempting to preclude making any connection. But the radicality of the focus in Christian hope does not place it in an isolation ward where it is given intensive care by theological nurses. "If the hope of faith is now directed toward a real historical future of God for man, then as hope in God it can no longer draw back from the concrete movements of hope by relegating their concerns with attainable goals and visible change to another kingdom, confronting them with apathy and indifference, and in this way simply coexisting with them." [40] All aspirations and actions for the transformation of the world demand response and engagement. An immunity born of arrogance implicitly negates the power of the future. All events that spring from the future in this sense rumor the coming of God.

While the future in the present is fragmentary and incomplete, ultimately the future of the world is singular and unitary. "The message of the coming Kingdom of God implies that God in his very being is the future of the world. All experience of the future is, at least indirectly, related to God himself. . . . Every event in which the future becomes finitely present must be understood as a contingent act of God. . . ." [41] To deny the authenticity or significance of futurological tendencies existing independent of Christian nomenclature is in effect to deny God as the power of the future. Present plurality does not negate ultimate unity. Modern futuristic movements may be differentiated from the future of God, but they ought not to

be disconnected from it. If Christians will not relate themselves to those transcending events in which modern men reach
beyond themselves, they preclude contact with the only form
of transcendence with which many can identify. Christians
would not only be removing themselves from where modern
man believes "the action is," but from the possibility of interaction with theological awarenesses. Both apologetically and in
terms of our understanding of reality, a futuristic eschatology
must be rigorously attentive to the lively hopes and joyful anticipations in our culture.

But apart from the imperative to make contact with and to
engage movements of human hope, what is the specific relationship of futuristic eschatology to them? Jürgen Moltmann
specifies two.[42] First, it must perform the uncomfortable and
unpleasant task of exposing "their uncritical naïveté." Illusion
permeates every human effort at establishing freedom and justice; often resignation is a correlative. Human hopes err both in
the direction of expecting too much and too little, often simul-
taneously. The quality of resignation erects boundaries and
narrows the future. Presumption enters at the point of a confidence in the quality and capacity of human nature that history
will never support. Christian eschatology performs a critical
function against human optimism, which assumes it can effect
man's reconciliation with his existence, and human pessimism,
which is created by the magnitude of evil in man and the
world. And it does so in the power of hopes "enacted on better
promises" (Heb. 8:6). Secondly, Christian eschatology must
serve as a catalyst that in the best sense exploits movements of
human hope, driving them beyond themselves. It must respond
expansively to the possibilities operative in the present, envi-
sioning how what is there and what could be there corresponds
to its own hope. Without accommodating to what is given and
persuasive in the moment, it is obligated to respond to emerging historical possibilities and to bring them into line with the
Christian hope. Thus it will be prepared to grasp the momen-
tum and vision present in the moment, even as it holds firm to
its own understanding of the future. It is not too proud to

make common cause with lesser hopes, yet it reaches for those levels of fulfillment that lie beyond them. Thus it is prepared to gather what is given into its own vision, graciously and not condescendingly, for what is given is related, if only fragmentarily, to the power of the future it affirms. Only then can the Biblical pictures of man and society seen through the prism of Christ affect the aspirations and achievements of man. In contrast to secular futurists, the proponents of futuristic eschatology are concerned, not with a becoming in history, but with a coming into history from the future. The future has been previewed in Jesus with his message of anticipation and the incarnation of it in his person.

In this chapter we have been exploring what it would mean to think of God as coming to us from the future. And that presents us with a different view of reality. Instinctively we think from the past through the present into the future. This linear posture is constricting. The future becomes a consequence of what has gone before and can be calculated on those terms. The alternative is to begin with the end, to perceive the future as what gives shape and form to the past and present. That vision of reality allows for radical openness and the possibility that there can be new and unpredictable events. When the reality of God is understood as in the future and God as himself the power of the future, then the possibilities are indeterminate. The consequences of this are substantial for the practice of hope. One can exist beyond cynicism in the assurance that the future is not an outgrowth of where we are and what we can do about it, but is a movement from God himself. And the present is something activated by God, who meets us in every moment with the realization that there are more options than we have any right to anticipate. Our freedom and our confidence are a function of One who is ahead of us and who promises, "I cause to be what I cause to be." The disposition to hope for the new is taken up into One for whom newness is the quality of his being.

# IV

# THE PARTIALITY OF GOD

Cynicism thrives on the contention that nothing really new is possible. What will be is an extension, if not a repetition, of what has been. The resulting sensibility is inertia and futility. The prospects of living beyond cynicism are created by a faith which sets the Christian message in focus on the public dimensions of human existence. It identifies in man the disposition to hope, which is made viable by understanding God as the power of the future. To say that God acts upon the present from the future, however, runs the risk of remaining an abstraction. We need now to press the argument toward specifying the peculiar form his presence assumes, the way in which he is with us as the One who is ahead of us.

## God Takes Sides

What is made inexorably clear in Jesus of Nazareth is the partiality of God. He takes sides unashamedly but, of course, revocably. Many would prefer to think of him as more judicious than that. A God who can be persuaded to the sidelines is safer. We can engage in rather painless "trade-offs" with a deity who doesn't position himself in history. But the God of the exodus and of the Crucified One risks impurity in history; he becomes partisan when the stakes are freedom. That context is, of course, a crucial qualification. It would be a distortion to think one could discern the stance of God on the full range of human problems. It does not render God remote to affirm that he does not relate to many issues. But he does cut through to the marrow where oppression is the condition and liberation the need. There God cannot be neutral. The Biblical story is a record of the sides he has taken. It becomes clear in the exodus event when God stands with the Israelites and against the Egyptians. A strangely inconsequential tribe of nomads, in effect runaway slaves, were chosen to initiate a process of liberation. God inaugurated a relationship that placed him unmistakably on one side and against another. That is precisely the way Israel remembered the event. The writer in Exodus recalls that God instructed Moses to remind his people in the wilderness of Sinai, "You have seen what I did to the Egyptians, and how I bore you on eagles' wings and brought you to myself" (Ex. 19:4). The prophetic tradition builds on that unlikely foundation. With an unattenuated sensitivity the prophets identified the crushing of the human spirit and proclaimed the identification of God with the losers of the world. They see "that it is the little people at the bottom who are God's levers of liberation. . . . He sides with the revolutionary opposition, using his voice and muscle in behalf of the poor, the oppressed, and the useless little people in the world." [43]

There is, then, a history of partisan activity with which Jesus connects. Once again in Christ God intrudes and sides with the oppressed. He makes their suffering and deprivation his own and instills the freedom to rebel. Jesus' message and ministry specify that the Kingdom belongs to the poor, while the rich are not likely to find access; his work is on behalf of the downtrodden and deprived, while the privileged bear the sting of his wrath; the balance in history will be tipped by the power of the powerless, while the powerful will become powerless; the authority of God does not coincide with the "principalities and powers" but with the victims of oppression who struggle to liberate themselves. It is striking indeed that when Jesus goes into the Temple and reads from Isaiah, he identifies the contours of his ministry as shaped by preaching "good news to the poor," not success to the wealthy, "release to the captives," not spoils to the captors, the recovery of "sight to the blind," not new visions to those who already see, and setting "at liberty those who are oppressed," not enhancing the position of those in power (Luke 4:18-19). The inception of his ministry was marked by a rejection of neutrality; Jesus made clear his determination to come down on one side and not another.

While liberation is clearly for all men, the process of liberation works against the posturing of the oppressors and for the freedom of the oppressed. We can best understand the community of Christians gathered by the resurrection of Jesus as a people committed to "the recital of liberating historical events . . . events which made man free, that made possible a now self-understanding so radical as to be called a 'new birth' (cf. Jn. 3:3), events which indicated that God was actively engaged in a struggle against the powers that kept man captive." [44] It is not too bold to equate Jesus' work with the deliverance of the oppressed.

What we have been saying about the Judeo-Christian tradition works against one of the prevailing critiques of faith in God. More than a few have argued that religion reduces human possibility and encourages accommodation. Ernst Bloch writes that "where there is a great master of the world there is no room for freedom" and goes on to contend that *"without atheism there is no room for messianism."* [45] The obvious assumption is that any deity is at odds with an affirmation of human freedom and a viable future. In our experience it is evident that masters are not the generators of indeterminate possibilities but the instigators of suppression. In the human realm authority tends to work against liberty, though not always. But the experience of the people of Israel and of the community which deals with Jesus is that theism is the only authentic base for messianism. Their confession is that they are never so free, the future is never so open, and history is never as susceptible to radical newness as when they are drawn into the politics of God.

Far from faith in God encapsulating man and anesthetizing his potential, it is the condition of liberation. The Israelites did not understand their deliverance as a function of their own initiative or as a convergence of favorable circumstances; freedom was something that was brought about by a force in their history. Liberation is the function of a Liberator who cannot let man make peace with oppression; the restoration of humanness and the inflation of the spirit is an act of God. The vectors in history which lance oppression and liberate man result from the activity of a God who is not afraid of partiality or the risks of identification in particular moments of time. Far from being the antithesis of freedom, God is the source of the process of transcendence through which man moves beyond himself. As the power of the future he is the ground of freedom and the guarantor of its prevailing against the forces of encapsulation. In Jesus we understand him as a different kind of God than those gods familiar to the secular realm; he comes in the form of a messiah suffering as a servant in the world. There we can identify with him. Indeed, the glory of God no longer enters the world through those who wear jeweled crowns but through those who wear crowns of thorns.

Liberation means setting the conditions whereby man can freely choose his own history. The oppressed are those who have never created their own history. They cannot get life going on their own terms; they are trapped by an agenda set for them. Freedom is not to be understood as boundarylessness; part of being free is to know the limit that the neighbor constitutes in my decisions. It is one thing to have every option and quite another to exercise every option without restraint. The free man accepts limits, but he chooses them freely! The oppressed are those who have lost transcendence in the sense that they are submerged either in the world processes or in their own self-indulgence. They cannot view their condition from a horizon and decide where they will cast their weight. The power to assess and initiate is dissipated.

Freedom means in the most radical sense being thrust against oneself with the responsibility of dealing with the future as it presses in on the present. "The course of liberation . . . is . . . not aimed at facilitating somnolence or generalizing the pleasureable, comfortable leisure of the contemporary upper classes. . . . The goal . . . is this: to give to every man . . . his own distress, boredom, wretchedness, misery, and darkness, his own buried, summoning light . . . so that he will be clear about himself." [46] Liberation aims at rendering man a subject in history rather than an object of history; the restoration of intentionality and its relation to visions is the goal. And it is to this condition that Jesus is most intimately connected. In the New Testament, Jesus is received as the Messiah because he sets sinners free and heals the sick. He lifts the burden of those who labor and are heavy laden; the rejected and reviled, the poor and hungry, are comforted and affirmed through him. Freedom from the anguish of death and the eclipse of hope emerges through his resurrection after death on the cross. Jesus is understood by the community of faith as reconstituting the self as an agent in history and enabling the anticipating consciousness to select from the future.

### Theology as Anthropology

One of the problems with which theology has wrestled is the question of whether Christianity should be interpreted as God-centered or man-centered. Where indeed does one begin in the exposition of the faith? Quite diverse theologians have called for "balance." Karl Barth admonished the theologian to fall asleep neither on his Bible nor his newspaper, but in the development of his *Church Dogmatics* he articulated the faith from the Word. Paul Tillich specified that one should correlate the eternal message of faith and the human condition as it was experienced at a given time; yet he was bold in beginning with an analysis of existence before naming the "answers" of faith. And the impression grow that while one calls for balance, some kind of a decision has to be made between doing theology or anthropology.

Now an alternative is to name the distinction as arbitrary and to see theology as anthropology. It hardly needs arguing that the Christian faith centers on God-talk. However ambiguous this might become, to presume to speak of the Christian faith apart from God is manifestly absurd. But it is equally false to presume that one can engage in talk about God apart from man. The initiative of God and the condition of man are given together; we have no access to God apart from his engagement in the predicament of man. One cannot speak of God as Liberator apart from man as oppressed; neither can one speak of man's oppression apart from the One who is the power of the future. To begin with God as Liberator or man as oppressed is a distinction without a difference. The definitive thing Christ does to our understanding of God is to establish indelibly the fusion of the action of God and the aspiration of man for freedom. There is no way in which we can speak of God or man separate from the intersection of liberation and oppression. Abstraction is no longer a possibility.

One of the few American theologians who have elected to operate in the framework we have been specifying is James H. Cone. He begins with the premise that "Christianity is essentially a religion of liberation. The function of theology is that of analyzing the meaning of that liberation for the oppressed community so that they will know that their struggle for political, social, and economic justice is consistent with the gospel of Jesus Christ." [47] The activity of God is by its nature liberating; he identifies with the bruised and humiliated in their struggle for freedom. He is the God of the oppressed. In our time this means that he is on the side of black people. The struggle of blacks to throw off white oppressors is the work of God. God is at work in the world through identification with black people, vindicating their movement and sustaining it as his will in the world.

This is not to argue that only blacks are oppressed. But they are a conspicuously visible reality that identifies what oppression is in America. Blackness for Cone is understood as an "ontological symbol" that represents every conceivable inhumane act and predicament. As such it specifies that reality in relation to which all theology must be articulated. But this black experience of oppression is not merely something to "keep in view" while one is thinking through the faith. It is the nexus within which the faith is formulated. The black experience is God's way of acting in America. This means that black power is not merely the black man's affirmation of himself and his determination to manage his own existence. In the measure that the gospel sets a man free to be for the oppressed of the world, then in our time the impact of black power and the message of Christ are synonymous. The determination of black people to carry out their own destiny is not alien to the gospel but at the heart of it.

Cone proceeds from the understanding of God as liberating black people in our time to the claim that he is in fact black. Not only is God disclosed in the situation of liberation, but he is totally identified with the black condition. God is black in that he makes the condition of oppression his own. Since the essence of God's activity is liberation, his engagement in history involves the risk of being totally on the side of the black struggle as he gave himself to the Israelites in bondage in Egypt and became himself the Oppressed One in Jesus of Nazareth. For Cone, it is in the nature of God not to bless good causes but to risk himself in them. He is not merely for liberation but totally immersed in it. And we have no access to him apart from this identification. One cannot bypass the black experience, symbolically understood, and deal with God. "People who want to know who God is and what he is doing must know who black people are and what they are doing. . . . Knowing God means being on the side of the oppressed." [48] It is in his blackness that God comes to us, and we can only receive his self-disclosure by becoming one with him in his work of liberation. To know God is to get on the side he is on in the struggle at hand.

It is a logical extension of understanding the blackness of God to affirm a black Christ. There is the question of who he is. This question is resolved in the context of where he is. In Christ, God took on the human condition of oppression and suffered it through to the cross. His birth in a stable, his baptism and temptation, the location of his ministry among the abused, and his overcoming death through the resurrection identify his presence in human liberation on all levels. We know him in the condition of oppression and the process of liberation. Who Christ is for us today is experienced existentially in the negation of oppression and the affirmation of liberation. Since the work of Jesus was carried out among the oppressed and at odds with the oppressors, and since he is to be found among the dispossessed and not in the power structure, we can only be true to the New Testament witness by understanding him as black. As God once became oppressed man in Jesus of Nazareth, he now becomes oppressed man in the person of black Americans. Indeed, according to Cone we cannot speak of the presence of Jesus apart from the liberation forces at work in the black community. The very concreteness of his continued incarnation is sustained by the concept of a black Christ. And for us now, to be "a man in Christ" is to be into what God is into: the liberation of blacks from their bondage to white America.

Professor Cone predicted that white theologians would be put off by the particularism in his stance. Black theologians as well often find it less than defensible. One writes, "We need not color God or the Christ black in order to appreciate blackness as an instrument of the Divine." [49] He argues the case on the basis of an idolatry of color. Yet this is indeed to miss the point. Cone acknowledges that black is an "ontological symbol." It stands for a condition which is the dominant experience of blacks, without being their exclusive possession. But more importantly, Cone argues that we must take dangerous risks in relating our experience in society with theology. When we test the Biblical record, it is rather clear that the action of God was and is on behalf of the oppressed. "Black theology says that as Father, God identified with oppressed Israel participating in the bringing into being of this people; as Son, he became the Oppressed One in order that all may be free from oppression; as Holy Spirit, he continues his work of liberation." [50] And what is significant is the absence of neutrality in the context of liberation. It is something God is for, not in principle but in particular. He comes down on one side and against another. In part, the legitimacy of this is in the fact that the condition of the oppressed is not as fraught with ambiguity as is that of the powerful. Between the United States and the Soviet Union one could not specify which side God is on; in the nature of the case, he is on neither side. But in the context of oppressed and oppressor, the ambiguity recedes. The real offense to the gospel is not the particularism evident in Cone but the abstraction in which much theology is formulated. Fidelity to the Incarnate One requires specificity in history.

James Cone has explained the meaning of the Christian faith from the perspective of the black community and its experience of oppression. He has in fact explicated God's liberating activity so that a particular people in a particular time at a particular place can experience the liberating forces in their lives as rooted in the power of the future. But some eighty-nine percent of us in America are not black! Rather boldly he admonishes us to become black. That is not something at which one "works." Far from being an accomplishment, it is a gift. The man of faith orients his existence around the presence of Christ in the oppressed black condition. Yet we need to remember that for Cone blackness is symbolic. Oppression overlaps most radically, but not exclusively, with the black community. The plight of blacks does not exhaust the symbol. We may have to understand oppression and liberation through the black experience, but its forms are inexhaustible. Cone does not argue, but neither would he deny, that liberation is "man's universal need. . . . It makes room for emancipation from both social customs and structures inherited from the past and from mental structures and attitudes imposed or insinuated by Western technological society. . . . In a sense, we are more in need of liberation than are materially oppressed and dominated peoples, because we are not aware of our subjection to tyrannical assumptions." [51] To be into what God is doing in Christ at this moment of history is to participate in the full range of bondages and link up with the freeing forces at work. The danger, of course, is that one will be everywhere—and nowhere effectively. Each man will need to make his own peace with that issue. What matters is to be part of God's awakening of man from his bondage and swept up in the freedom forces.

## Liberation and Futurelessness

When we understand God as the power of the future, we can understand his work as standing against all the forces of futurelessness we find in ourselves, others, and the structures of society. The lives of the oppressed are no longer opened to the world. And that includes the oppressors. The oppression of the oppressors is thick and demonic. While God does not take sides with them, his freeing of their slaves may finally translate into a freeing of the masters. When Jesus said of his sheep, "I came that they may have life, and have it abundantly" (John 10:10), he was identifying a process of liberation that was intended to restore a future to all men. The essential meaning of being alive is to experience openness to the future. One of the spin-offs from the partiality of God can be the restoration of humanity to the inhumane. It may not be the intent of black theology to liberate whites, but that may be the effect. In the Biblical tradition God is everywhere and always involved in history, effecting the form that human existence assumes. That is why a new order is expected, one that supports and sustains the struggle of every life to be really human. To affirm that God takes sides does not preclude liberation for the oppressors.

The political and religious establishment in Old Testament times referred to the prophets as those "troublers of Israel." With their acute aversion to inhumane acts, the prophets challenged the morals and mores of their era. They not only troubled the comfortable but developed a sense of their own distress among the victims of society. Jesus stands in that tradition and fulfills it unreservedly. He causes men to be discontent with their discontent. The presence of Christ is inherently a threat to the oppressors and a nutriment to the rebellious impulses of the oppressed. He awakens the determination in man to negate the negations of his being and align himself with the forces and movements for freedom.

Faith in Christ does not translate into peace with the world but into agitation against the powers which constrict the human spirit. "When Christians discover themselves as the rebels, as a part of the 'Great Refusal,' as those who cannot adapt, as the disturbers of prevailing order, they are not, therefore, betraying a tradition of conformism and passivity but rather recovering what is most fundamental and primordial in the history and consciousness of the community of faith." [52] They have a vocation for freedom that roots in God as the power of the future. Inevitably, that mission leads one into contradictions of the ways in which life is ordered in society. Paul and Silas came up against that when they made their way into Thessalonica. The charge was formulated early, indeed, before they had done more than walk about the city: "These men who have turned the world upside down have come here also . . . and they are . . . acting against the decrees of Caesar, saying that there is another king, Jesus" (Acts 17:6-7). The impact of Jesus and his message is not intoxication but fermentation. It leads to revolt against all conditions that prevent man from having a history of his own. It instills visions of a new day that contradict the day at hand. It causes man to inhale the future and exhale the past. By any measure, Jesus is an agent of distress.

## Jesus and the Revolutionaries

When we understand the work of Christ as essentially liberation, it is important that we consider his relationship to revolutionary movements of his time. Theoretically, at least, that will save us from reading into our understanding of him our need for sanctions in the midst of movements for radical change. Fundamental to this consideration is a judgment

about the relation of Jesus to the Zealots and the degree to
which he might have been involved with a Jewish resistance
movement against the Roman rule. It is not likely that anyone
will argue effectively that Jesus was a Zealot; some, however,
may depict him as bordering on being a fellow-traveler in that
movement, while others will contend his effect and intent were
more a revolution of individual consciousness.

The first option is embraced by S. G. F. Brandon in his remarkable study, *Jesus and the Zealots*. Brandon is intent upon
reconstituting an image of Jesus that will thrust him more directly into current "religion and politics" tensions. The obvious
import of this is to rescue Jesus from the abstraction of doctri-
nal disputes about his nature, the piety which leads to arid in-
dividualism, and an ethic which dissolves into privatism. Brandon accomplishes this goal by establishing that while Jesus was
not himself a Zealot, his own teachings and ministry were compatible with the movement. This is not to argue that in any
sense Jesus personally engaged in a resistance movement
against Rome; but, unlike the Scribes and Pharisees, he never
repudiated the Zealots. He sympathized with their cause
without being a card-carrying member. To establish his case,
Brandon proceeds to point out the accommodation Mark made
in the light of the precarious position in which the Christians
of Rome found themselves. In order to survive in any viable
way as a community, it was important for the Christians to be
understood as disciples of a figure who was victimized by Jewish leaders. Mark depoliticized Jesus. The other Gospel writers
essentially followed his lead. But the evidence in favor of understanding Jesus as radically challenging the political and religious authority of the day escapes this cover-up. For all the at-
tempts to picture Pilate as a reluctant participant in a Jewish
plot, "the most certain thing known about Jesus of Nazareth is
that he was crucified by the Romans as a rebel against their
Government in Judea." [53] It was clear to Pilate that the actions of Jesus were essentially seditious and that the direct consequences of his ministry threatened the established rule of
Rome. His condemnation to death was consistent with other

facts in the record that point toward Jesus' pro-Zealot tendencies. Jesus did not hesitate to include an acknowledged Zealot in his inner circle of disciples. While the inclusion of Simon suggests that Jesus himself was not a Zealot, it also establishes that Zealot principles were not an anathema to him or his mission. Jesus' attack on the Temple trading system was by any measure a challenge to Roman rule through the high priest, whose position and authority were a function of political power. This revolutionary act would surely have been applauded by the Zealots. Jesus shared the Zealots' commitment to the sovereignty of God over Israel, which was the basis of their opposition to the ultimate allegiance required by the state. He identified the first commandment as that of singularity in love of Israel's God (Mark 12:30). The only point where Jesus appears to have differed with the Zealots is that he was more disposed to attack the "sacerdotal aristocracy" of the Jews than the political hierarchy of the Romans. The net impact of Brandon's work is to flesh out a picture of Jesus as an eschatological figure whose ministry and teachings translated into conflict with the claims of the political order. While not a Zealot, the overlap of this resistance movement and Jesus' life and death is remarkable.

Oscar Cullmann wrestles somewhat more cautiously with the Zealot issue and moves toward conclusions that affirm the revolutionary aspects of Jesus' ministry while modifying them through a radical eschatology. Cullmann shares with Brandon a concern to make fruitful for our times the activity and sayings of Jesus while sustaining fidelity to his fundamental attitude. It is dangerous to speak to the issues of our time as Christians before we have resolved the historical problems of the way in which Jesus related to the movements and problems of his. The danger is exploitation by the ascription of our own posturing in history to Jesus. Cullmann has little doubt that Jesus was thought to be a Zealot, his death being directly related to that assumption. Given the situation in Palestine, where rebellion was rife against the Roman occupation forces, anyone causing apparent agitation would be viewed as one of the "resistance fighters." Roman responsibility for the condemnation of Jesus is supported both by the crucifixion as the form of death utilized by the Roman government and by the title placed over the cross, which pointed to a political crime. But the perceptions of the political establishment do not determine the truth of Jesus' ministry; they do not establish his connection with the Zealots.

Cullmann identifies two strains in the New Testament that witness in apparently contradictory directions.[54] One set of sayings and narratives suggests Jesus' close connection with Zealotry. Like the Zealots, Jesus emphasized the imminence of the Kingdom of God and saw himself as significantly related to its implementation; critical of Herod in particular, Jesus shared the Zealots' sensitivity to the oppressive rule of kings; certain of Jesus' sayings affirm the possession of weapons, and by implication associate him with the armed resistance that the Zealots advocated; Jesus included at least one Zealot in his inner circle and appeared to be carrying out a Zealot-like protest when he cleansed the Temple. Yet, at least as many texts can be brought forward which argue for Jesus' being an opponent of political resistance. While the Zealots had no qualms about violence, Jesus at times advocated nonviolence. The love of one's enemy, the blessedness of peacemakers, and the exhortation not to draw the sword reflect a style at odds with that of the Zealots. Jesus had a faithfulness to the Law that was not shared by the Zealots. A respectable Zealot would not have associated with establishment types, much less have incorporated a tax collector into his movement. Then too, Jesus' considerable caution in relation to political titles and activities worked against the primary activity of the Zealots.

Now while Cullmann affirms the importance of sustaining both these traditions, and rejects those who discredit one or the other, his real intent is to rise to the complexity in Jesus' relationship with his environment. One does not have to choose between the simplistic alternatives of Jesus as a revolutionary or as a defender of existing institutions. Both strains in the New Testament derive from Jesus' radical eschatology, the centrality of his future hopes. Thinking the end was near, he could sustain a bifocal vision. Jesus' allegiance was beyond all the realities of this world, and they were therefore relativized; yet his willingness to work with what was given was not a sanction of them. Cullmann supports this thesis as he looks at three questions. The question of worship focuses on Jesus' cleansing of the Temple. That act can be read as compatible with Zealotry, but it clearly falls short of the willingness of these "resistance fighters" to utilize force in destroying the operation. And Jesus does not share the determination of the Zealots to overthrow the entire Temple and priestly organization. God would take care of the destruction of the Temple. He was willing to operate within its framework for the time that remained. On the social question Jesus' judgment of the social order was revolutionary in terms of inequities, but again he was not committed to overthrowing that order. He exhorted his followers to implement the norms of the coming Kingdom, but again through a reform of existing institutions. Jesus brought social injustice under judgment and called for a change of heart in man's relation to God and one's neighbor. But all of this is within the context of the coming Kingdom, where God will deal with earthly structures. On the political question, Cullmann concludes that Jesus was crucified as a Zealot, but this does not identify his true relationship to that movement. "A careful investigation of Jesus' attitude to the political question of his day proves, on the contrary, that his condemnation was the result of judicial error." [55] There is no evidence that Jesus regarded himself as a political messiah; indeed, he preferred the title Son of Man. The temptation narratives reflect his determination to separate himself from the political connotations in messiahship. Cullmann concludes that, while Jesus was critical of the state, he accepted its existence on the assumption that it would disappear with the coming Kingdom.

   For Cullmann, Jesus was no Zealot; neither did he align himself with the Zealots' resistance movement. He was more concerned with inner conversion than institutional revolution. Governed by eschatological radicalism, he could be unreserved in his criticism of the existing order and yet reject resistance movements that presumed to implement the Kingdom that God alone could bring.

While Cullmann and Brandon overlap at certain points, they clearly divide at a crucial one: Brandon identifies a Christ who risks direct intrusion into the political arena without making a party alignment, while Cullmann identifies a Christ so intent upon the coming Kingdom that he centers on changing individuals without overthrowing institutions.

How shall we understand Christ in his time? And how shall we translate the scope of his liberating activity in our time? It would seem that Brandon and Cullmann differ more in degree than in kind. Clearly they agree on Jesus' impact. In his time, Jesus was experienced as a threat. The structures of the world —political, social, religious—were challenged radically by the claims of a coming Kingdom. "His life has engendered the closest thing to a permanent revolution which the world has ever known. And that same life in first century Palestine was not only regarded as subversive, seditious, and revolutionary, but it must have been genuinely so." [56] The degree to which his intentions were to affect institutions is another issue. Cullmann certainly comes down on the side of caution, while Brandon is prepared to risk some significant overlap with the Zealot movement. Their difference is in the extent to which Jesus' convictions about the present order were qualified by his anticipation of the Kingdom. The point may be more subtle than significant; perhaps it is academic, since immediacy in anticipation of the Kingdom has been relaxed by the passage of time.

There is no way we can discern the politics of Jesus or reconstruct his intentions. Both Brandon and Cullmann expose a Christ who made no peace with the oppressive forces operative in the world and who embodied the intention of God to open man to his future. "What we encounter in the Gospels is not a particular political strategy or an outdated revolutionary stance, but Jesus himself, the perennial Lord of the poor, the prisoners, the dispossessed, the harlots and tax gatherers and sinners." [57] And that, for all the world, is the partiality of God.

# V

# THE FUTURISTIC COMMUNITY

Man's disposition to hope is awakened and sustained within a community. The anticipating consciousness is not a consequence of individual aspirations. The expectation of something new is sustained by a people who live together under the promises of God. The reality of hope has a social construction. As Peter Berger writes: "Men are social beings. . . . Most of what we 'know' we have taken on the authority of others, and it is only as others continue to confirm this 'knowledge' that it continues to be plausible to us." [58] The community does not invent the future, but relating to it is a function of socializing processes. While what one hopes is defined by the future, abiding in hope requires social support. The Biblical events in which the promises of God were mediated not only happened to a community but were remembered in various forms of corporate acts. Men of faith sustained loyalty to hope in the presence of a hoping community. The appropriation of hope is never in isolation but always within a community that exists from the promises of God.

## The Corporate Context

God called the people of Israel and the church into being by the promise that he would be ahead of them. Too often the church is understood as the community that remembers what lies behind it. "The Church," writes Karl Barth, "is our common attempt to remember our God. We remember the Lord when we preach and hear the sermon. We remember the Lord when . . . we celebrate the Lord's Supper. . . . We remember the Lord when we sing . . . the hymns of our hymnals and when we read the Bible." [59] To be sure, without remembering there would be no anticipating. But to construct the life of the church solely around the process of remembering deprives it of dynamism. It puts the community of faith in the position of prolonging Christ in history rather than expecting him in history. In the context of hope, the church is the community of the second coming. It not only centers in the One who came but in the One who comes again. While the church was founded in response to the power of the future present in the Christ event, it continues to exist from the confidence that the future is still coming. It is certainly consistent with the Biblical writings to say that "the coming of Christ is every bit as much future as it is past." [60] Whatever else may be sustained in the image of the second coming, its central thrust points in the direction of a new event in a new future. The promises of God have not been exhausted or fulfilled. The church is the community that abounds in the hope that the One who came comes again. It lives "between the times" as they embrace the present conditions.

Now the Christ who comes again is expected by the church, but in the world. The church is a community of hope whose function is to frame the future of the world within the horizons of faith. The church embraces the world as the point of impact for its vision of the future. Jesus' message is not about the future of the church but about the church in relation to the future of the world. What distinguishes the church from the world is its consciousness of a destiny that transcends present conditions or extrapolations from past experiences. This is not its superiority but its vocation; its special understanding of the future is not a matter of privilege but of responsibility. Its purpose is to identify for all mankind the presence of God's future, to recognize the anticipatory signals that point to the destiny of the world. In this sense, the church is

the servant of the world. It calls the world to live by the promises of a new future that work against the present conditions.
But while the church has no life apart from the world, it dare
not find its life in the world. God as the power of the future
present in Jesus of Nazareth forces the community of faith into
history; but there must not be a merger of the hopes of the gospel and the hopes of the world. The future of God is in history
but is not of history. And the community of faith points to the
future as coming rather than as having arrived; it cannot compromise its horizon by identifying the future with any present
fulfillments.

This means that by virtue of its mission to the world the
church is an antagonizing community. "It is that world of men
who try to live from the promised future of God, and who,
from this perspective, call in question every world which tries
to understand itself only on the basis of its present and its own
possibilities." [61] The church intensifies the conflicts of the
world by its relating of the world to the promised future. Its
mission is not to provide relief from reality but to gather into
its own horizon existing impulses for reshaping man's social
and political existence. By virtue of its attention to the future
it gets in the way of making peace with the present. Refusing
to be a place where men steady themselves in the midst of
change, or secure themselves against it, it is the initiator of discontent.

To the degree that it injects hope, the church creates a consciousness that works against the way things are, that cannot
put up with reality as it is. When it teaches vision it instills
disillusionment. The community of hope is a people whose
message provokes imagination and arouses anticipation; it en-
genders the zeal to implement hope in the sociopolitical structures of existence. Nothing is more disquieting than the intrusion of the future into a comfortable and orderly present. The
church is true to its mission when it holds its passion for the
future against the forms of futurelessness in the world. It provokes and disturbs in faithfulness to its visions and anticipations of a new day. To the degree that it becomes an enclave

for changelessness, it is no longer the church of Jesus Christ but a sanctified section of the world.

In the context of hope, it is not the function of the individual in lonely splendor to speak the critical word in the social order. To be sure, God has always raised up prophets who spoke the word of judgment. But they were functions of a hoping community, even if the quality of hope had waned at a given moment. The church as a community must speak from the vantage point of the future to the situation at hand. Faith is invariably institutionalized, and the responses in history must be those of the church as an institution. The Christian belongs to a people who hope, and it is their common anticipations that work back into the present. Albert Camus had a strangely Biblical understanding of enacting the claims of the future in the present as a community: "What the world expects of Christians is that Christians should speak out, loud and clear, and that they should voice their condemnation in such a way that never a doubt, never the slightest doubt, could arise in the heart of the simplest man. That they should get away from abstraction and confront the bloodstained face that history has taken on today. The grouping we need is a grouping of men resolved to speak out clearly and to pay up personally." [62] While men inevitably pay up individually, they speak out collectively.

The future draws men together through the promises of God and they stand together against futurelessness in the world. Of course, there is a sense in which institutions by their nature tend to be uncritical. Being formations in the present, they tend to be sanctions of it. But to the degree that the church lives from the future it is a "counter culture." And it is renewed and reconstituted in its relationship to the future by the One who not only came but comes again. This is not to deny that it can become preoccupied with trivial discriminations. There are pressures that would make it a bastion of futurelessness. But the One who is the power of the future cannot leave it alone; God restores the church as the community that lives from the promises. This renewal of the church is not a spiritual renewal in the sense of piety; it is renewal in the sense of drawing the church into conflict with the forms of oppression in the world.

## The Church and Partiality

Wolfhart Pannenberg writes that "the Church has the task of demythologizing the political myths of a given time and of sobering up those who have become drunk on their possession of power." [63] The mission of the church is to expose the political formations that work against freedom, especially where it is being deceitfully professed. Its witness to a future fulfillment calls in question the illusions of "success" and inspires visions of new possibilities. This is not to say that the church disdains heritage and tradition. Both can be the source of freedom and the guarantee of its being perpetuated. But to the degree that they no longer remain open to the future or codify the past, the church is obligated to demythologize and expose the pretensions.

In the previous chapter we argued the partiality of God. The church as futuristic community follows the lead of the One who is the power of the future. It is not a body of mystics who strive to enjoy God apart from the world; neither is it an enclave for antiquarians who want to relive the past in all its sacred splendor. It is a people who strive to participate in what God is doing in the world to make and keep human life human. That requires the risk of radical identification with the oppressed. It is possible that James Cone is too restrictive when he defines the church as the community of the oppressed who participate in Jesus' action for liberation. That certainly would be true for blacks; as a race their experience is one of oppression. But the implication that the church could only be a community of the oppressed narrows the scope too drastically. The distinction called for is between seeing the church as a body of the oppressed and seeing the church as a people who assume the condition of oppression through their identification with the oppressed. In other words, while oppression may not be a precondition for becoming the church, it is certainly a consequence of being the church.

It is the task of the church to become one with the powerless in their struggle for time and space in which to be human. The only way in which it can deliver good news to the poor, release to the captives, and restoration of sight to the blind is through sharing as its own the conditions of poverty, captivity, and blindness. Benevolence from the sidelines is not an option for a community energized by the power of the future. It is driven not only into history but into solidarity with the hurting edges of the world. Liberation can only be achieved from within the condition of oppression; it cannot be encouraged by well-meaning bystanders who shout encouragement. Concretely, the futuristic community "believes in, and lives on the basis of, a reality of liberation that is not recognized by the ruling class. The church is that community which refuses to accept things as they are and rebels endlessly against the humiliation and oppression of man. It is the community through which the oppressed One has chosen to make his will known to the world. It is a liberating community whose chief task is to be to the world that visible possibility of God's intention for man." [64] To be aligned with Christ in the world is to be on the side of the oppressed, where the liberating action is to take place. Christ identifies for the church its place in the world and the forces with which it is to make common cause.

To the degree that the church exercises loyalty to hope, it is a suffering people. Bonhoeffer's point about being a Christian can be extended to the community of faith: to be the church is to participate in the suffering of God in the life of the world. The church recognizes that "in order to participate in the politics for a new tomorrow it is necessary to participate in the sufferings of today. . . . The community of the future, therefore, does not discover its futurity because of an esoteric knowledge of the world of the future, but rather from its identification with the sufferings of the slaves, the outcasts, the hopeless and futureless man, weak and impotent, the wretched of the earth." [65] God suffers as long as the conditions that prevail do not correspond with the promises he has made. And the church is that community which makes the suffering of God its own as it relates to the conditions of men. To know God is to know him in the pain of his being as he struggles against, and is crucified by, the powers of the world. The church lives its knowledge of God in the world.

Certainly a case can be made for identifying the church with the processes of reconciliation; some use that as a base from which to resist the image of the church as a liberating wedge in the world. But the issue which gets confused in that assertion is, reconciliation with what? The answer, of course, is reconciliation with God, which does not then mean accommodation with the world. Reconciliation has nothing to do with a people who have learned "to get along." The church is a community of people who cannot "make do" in the world as it is. To be straight with God is to participate in his being unreconciled with a world which defuturizes men. Because of its understanding of reconciliation, the futuristic community is a body which cannot be reconciled cheaply but only through suffering identification with all the forms and experiences of futurelessness.

What distinguishes the church from other institutions and equips it for the risks in identification, is that it need not be concerned with its own future. It is free from the need for self-preservation. When true to its coming Lord, the church's commitment to the horizon of the future preempts concern with its own future on the horizon. It has a healthy sense of its own provisionality. "For here we have no lasting city, but we seek the city which is to come" (Heb. 13:14). To the degree that it lives from and for the future, self-perpetuation is not a concern. It lives for what is coming and can therefore risk everything in the present as it seeks to implement what the future rule of Christ means at the moment. Because of the seriousness with which the church takes the coming Kingdom it can never take itself all that seriously. When it understands itself as "a section of humanity in which Christ has really taken form," [66] it no longer has to calculate how it is doing as an institution. It lives to die.

In the recognition of its own provisionality the church exposes the relativity of all institutions and the alliances it makes with persons, issues, and organizations. Identification is not deification. The church does not parcel out the sacred. In taking sides it gives provisional sanction but not sanctification. Jürgen Moltmann once commented that revolutionaries soon learn that Christians can't be trusted. They take sides radically, but they also change sides. The forces of liberation and the victims of oppression do not stay aligned in the same ways. The church may become identified with the struggle for freedom of one given people, only to bring that people under judgment as it achieves freedom and itself becomes an oppressor. It is legitimate for James Cone to draw an equation between the black people in their struggle for liberation and the work of God in the world. Yet the futuristic community might well have to withdraw its identification and from the critical distances established by its vision of the future name blacks as oppressors. The forces of futurelessness can be embodied in those who have emerged from that condition.

The problem of the world in which the church lives is that it has lost its horizon. Its efforts are always directed toward building to a future rather than living from the future. It is obsessed with its own self-creation, preservation, and realization. This world functions without a sense of the possibilities the future can bring, because it anxiously struggles to save itself through skills and organization; it is not free for the future because of its concentration on managing the present. Without an authentic horizon, it reels between the illusions of self-realization and the despair of self-estrangement. There is, of course, a propensity to hope; but that hope is more often in elements of experience which can be prolonged forward. Confidence emerges from such slogans as, "America has never lost a war," "Trust good old American ingenuity to come through," "Democracy is the greatest form of government in history." Expectations exist, but they tend not to be transcending ones; they arise out of history but do not call forth history. On those terms, the world cannot realize its possibilities or deal with its disillusionments. "The glory of self-realization and the misery of self-estrangement alike arise from hopelessness in a world of lost horizons. To disclose it to the horizon of the future of the crucified Christ is the task of the Christian Church." [67] Its responsibility to the world is to relate the futuristic dimension through which the world's limits become its possibilities.

But in order for the church to function in this way, it must itself be a community of prefiguration. In its own life it must point beyond the calculation of options in the present to the possibilities of the future. There must be within the community faithful embodiments of what is coming. The church which expects Christ to come again must live as if he were coming again. It will be an authentic futuristic community to the degree that it practices hope as a people. In every moment it will seek to implement the faith that God is ahead of them, calling a people to leave behind the securities of family and place and to strike out, not knowing where they are to go. It will gravitate to the centers of pain and work against them in the name of a better hope. It will be strangely free to love, because the future draws one into the lives of others in the way the past forbids. It will be prepared to risk everything, because it has nothing in itself that it is obligated to preserve. It will be known for a foolishness that makes folly of worldly wisdom. The world will be affected by the horizon of faith in the measure that it is prefigured in the life of the church.

## The Restoration of Hope

While the church is called to be a self-sacrificing community, it cannot merely exhaust itself in the world. It must nourish itself in hope in order to signal and commend it. The church needs an internal life through which it sustains itself in relation to the horizon of the future. This is not to advocate the cultivation of a sanctuary from the world but one for the world. The church can fulfill its mission of disclosing the horizon of the future only if through rite and ritual it confirms its own posture. In its corporate worship the church rehearses hope and sets itself toward the future with anticipations of something new. In the various acts of worship the church remembers in the form of hope and it hopes in the form of remembering. The act of communion clearly is a memorial service that relates us to the last supper Jesus had with his disciples. But what the community of faith remembers reaches back to his death from the perspective of his resurrection. That has a futurizing impact. Remembrance arouses anticipation and anticipation arouses memory. "In Holy Communion we declare that we are leaving the old world behind in joyful anticipation of the new. What we celebrate is the birth of newness, the new life in Christ, the presence of the Spirit as the guarantee of the promised goal, and the vision of the new world that is coming to man." [68] Those who gather around the communion table ought not to look as if they had lost their best friend; what the celebration of communion really means is the affirmation of the Lord of the future. The bread is broken and the wine poured in memory of Christ's sacrifice, but also in anticipation of his coming again. This is the way in which the futuristic community affirms the Christ who comes again and reigns between the times.

In the act of preaching, the church sets the tension between the promises of God and the present realities in the world. Preaching exposes the distance between possibilities and actualities. From the horizon of the future, it stabs every futureless motif and embodiment in the present. Preaching packs the social structures with explosives. It is the practice of political theology. But before the faith is translated into its worldly implications, the community of faith must be nourished in hope. And preaching is one of the forms in which the promises of God are mediated. It must hold up such samples of fulfillment as are available in the Biblical records and the life of the church through the ages. Preaching is the "verbal prolepsis of the new world" and as such provides "the driving wedge of the power of God's future in the depths of existence and the processes of history." [69] Its purpose is to awaken the sense of anticipation for something new through the promises of God and his faithfulness to them. It is in hearing the promise of a "new heaven and a new earth" that the Christian begins to identify what structures and pressures in the present he must lean his weight against.

Some will argue that there isn't much comfort in setting the tension between the promises and the realities. There isn't, if comfort means accommodation. But what greater word of comfort is there than that the way things are is not the way things are going to be? It may set the individual and the church to unpleasant tasks, but with a confidence and joy that exceed any forms of peace with the world one might otherwise achieve. True comfort comes when expectations are aroused and one functions in the confidence that the power of the future is present in the moment at hand.

Within a community that understands itself from the horizon of the future even the most private form of worship becomes a form of nurture in hope. Prayer is offered within the church through the Christ who comes again. It is through a coming Lord, not a dead hero, that prayers are formed. For prayer is a means through which we see our condition in history, and the conditions of others, against the promises of God in Christ. Prayer is not an exercise in which we hold God accountable for his promises. That is to presume God needs our prompting to make good on his word. "In prayer we hold the unredeemed face of this world up to the picture of God's promised future, and wrestle with him in the agony of the contradiction." [70]

The burden of prayer is to hold ourselves against the promises of God in the midst of the conditions that prevail— and that as surely in our private lives as in our public lives. In those moments that test most radically our capacity to cope, the act of prayer is a means of recalling what the promises of God are and allowing ourselves to be called forward toward their fulfillment. Even when the prayer is a shout of protest, it is laid against the possibilities of the future. All the traditional forms of prayer are exercises in hope. The prayer of confession is an acknowledgment that our loyalty to hope has wavered; the prayer of intercession is a holding of hope against the present on behalf of another; the prayer of thanksgiving is a rejoicing in hope legitimated in our experience; the prayer of petition is for the strength to stand firm in hope ourselves. The person who prays hopes and the person who hopes prays.

## The Impact of the Future

The church sustains itself in hope through its acts of worship and equips itself for its life in the world. But this focus on hope has other internal consequences. The verification of the gospel in the world through attention to the promises will have the effect of drawing the churches together. Both laymen and professionals are weary of the ecumenical movement. At times, all it seems to accomplish is a refocusing of the issues that divided Christians in the first place. These matters will not be resolved by a perpetual rehashing of the theological issues. The most that often comes of such activity is compromises that make everyone uneasy. But the unity of the church may be found in the world as the church seeks to implement the future of hope. The people of God cannot find one another through speculative processes. But they can embrace one another through a unity of the spirit as they practice hope together. To the degree that the churches find Christ in the liberating processes operating in the world, and align themselves with them, they have an authentic prospect of finding their own unity. Only a vision of reality in the future driving one to the practice of hope in the present can overcome the centuries of division. It is the church's very passion for the future that enhances its own prospects for renewal and reunification.

And to broaden that point, it can be said that the futuristic community experiences judgment against itself by virtue of its loyalty to hope. The horizon of the future for the world also bends back against the community of faith. The church is exposed by the presence of God's future. The message of the gospel calls the community in question; it is tested as hope is injected into its own life. The message of the coming Kingdom interrogates the church. It questions its earthly alliances and accommodations, it raises the issue of privatized faith versus political consciousness, it calls the community out of secure sanctuaries and sets before it new risks, it drives the church against the forms of futurelessness within its own midst, it holds the formulations of faith up for examination, it sets creativity in style and worship against form and conformity, it searches out its practices that may sanction oppression explicitly or implicitly. In the process of disclosing to the world the horizon of the future revealed in Christ, the church is caused to investigate itself with respect to lost horizons. Hope, then, is always the hope of the church, even as the church is a community of hope.

There are those who are saying that the church has overextended itself in the world. Its preoccupation with sociopolitical realities has led to a deadening of the spirit and an immunity to the private forms of human need. Certainly the cross of Jesus was a very public event, including the processes that led up to crucifixion; but for many it is a very personal experience in their lives. When and if it is the case that a particular community of faith is so directed by its public consciousness that it has no individual sensitivity, it works from a very narrow understanding of hope. A political theology may take a public target, but it aims for the conditions that will enable the individual to possess his possibilities and flesh out in freedom his humanity. The presence of the future redeems life for the person even as it concentrates on structures; it works against the church's becoming a pious enclave unrelated to the world in which God is at work. But that does not mean it is immune to the private forms of hurting that individuals experience. The futuristic community is a place of healing by virtue of its affirmation of God as the power of the future. Visions of the future, the

arousal of imagination, the creation of an anticipating consciousness are as relevant to our private lives as they are to our
public lives. The eschatological horizon understood through
the crucified and risen Christ speaks to the conditions of death,
guilt, meaninglessness with a word of promise that alone can
heal. It is a false dichotomy, then, when the community of
faith is called to choose between social engagement and private
nurture.

The church need not cease to be a community responsive to
personal needs because of public commitments. In fact, the
church tends to renew itself as it practices hope in the world.
Harvey Cox may be only overstating a truth when he claims
that "renewal of the church happens only when the church re-
sumes political apostolate. Whether we look at the East
Harlem Protestant Parish, the Iona Community in Scotland,
the worker-priests of France, or the Roman Catholic revolutionaries in Latin America, wherever we find new life in the
church we find political engagement." [71] Public concern is only
an intensified form of concern for the person; the church with
a political consciousness will be one with heightened sensitivity
to the individual.

The only authentic and durable stance against cynicism is
one sustained by a community responsive to God as the power
of the future. The church fulfills its mission in the measure
that it focuses its vision of the future upon the present conditions in the world. Its manner of waiting for the future is the
practice of hope through faithful embodiments of what is to
come.

# VI

## THE PROLEPTIC LIFE-STYLE

The practice of hope requires a deprivatized faith. The possibility of living beyond cynicism emerges when the Gospel is interpreted with reference to the public formations of our existence. While addressing man in society, the Christian faith connects with his disposition to hope. He is a creature who experiences authenticity in the aspiration for a new future. Man the "hope-er" is not, however, a lonely dreamer. He is sustained by God as the power of the future who overcomes in the present the forces of futurelessness. The peculiar form of his presence is on the side of the oppressed. In Jesus of Nazareth we see that God wedges himself in history on behalf of freedom movements. But the process of hope, as well as the substance of things hoped for, is sustained within a community. The church is the people of God practicing hope together.

This summary of our argument comes to rest finally upon the individual and the way in which he implements hope in his personal life. That dimension has been latent in previous chapters, but it is now our task to develop it explicitly. Yet one cannot go directly to the issue of life-style. From within the Christian faith it does not stand on its own as a program or as a profile to be achieved. A person within the faith puts himself together around a center. Life-style is a response, a function of a controlling vision. The image I find most demanding and fulfilling as a center from which to act out the faith is that of a suffering God.

## The Suffering God

While it is fundamental to understand the reality of God as in the future and to identify him as the power of the future, it is not sufficient. Clearly it links him with our most demanding aspirations; that is a connection one dare not take lightly. A man lives by and in his hopes. We do indeed make contact with the man of our age when we set before him "the hope that is in us." But talk of hope does not fully take possession of us until it embraces explicitly our experience of the present against which hope works. What we anticipate is a contradiction of what exists now. And we need an understanding of God that dramatizes his identification with our plight. It is most persuasive if we can recognize in God's experience what we know to be true of our own. Thus, the correlative to hope in God is his suffering.

Christians have tended to be uncomfortable with the image of a suffering God. It is almost as if we would think better of him if he were above it. Some feel the need to think of God without blemish; they cannot take into their understanding of God any qualities that could be read as weakness. To acknowledge suffering in God would compromise his deity. But the Biblical faith will not support human efforts to immunize God against the human condition. The very meaning of the incarnation is that he made it unalterably his own; the cross certifies that he did not pull back in the moment of crisis. God suffers as the Father of the Son he offers. The Christ event is one of self-giving. Beginning in Bethlehem and ending on Golgotha, it is saga of love and pain. Suffering is not an anathema to God, but the consequence of his involvement as the power of the future operative in the present. And the resurrection of Jesus was not a way out, for he remains both the crucified One and the risen One. Christian hope rests on both the resurrection as the power of God and the cross as the suffering of God in the world.

The cross establishes the credentials of God; it demonstrates his willingness to take the risks of existence into his own being. Suffering is not something he happens into but is "a dimension of God";[72] it is not merely a reality of man and the world but a reality in God. Yet we need to move through the contention that he is a suffering God to explore why it is God suffers. Our temptation is to be fixed on the theodicy question, the problem of affirming God and acknowledging evil. Undergirding an answer to that must be an understanding of why God gets himself into the position of suffering. That will not resolve the question of why man suffers, but it will give it a context. And, one hopes, it will establish as well his viability as One in whom we can really hope.

We can begin to understand the suffering of God with the recognition that love and pain are given together. Our impulse may well be to associate love and joy; indeed, we know the positive sensations that accompany an act of love. But it may be more important to understand that suffering is a form of love. Certainly we can risk saying that "suffering is the authentic expression and communication of love." [73] Suffering is the price of involvement with human need. When one takes the condition of another to himself, there is a cost factor. We should not be afraid to say that love is a burden. Proof enough of that is the consistency with which we resist it. When we think of it as a feeling, we do its dimensions an unjustice. Love is a commitment, a responsibility, and it cannot escape the indemnity that comes of identification with the full range of another's experience. To love is to become vulnerable. No one has loved deeply or truly who has not known excruciating pain. Participation is a requisite for love, and those who risk it cannot escape suffering. The cross expresses the presence of God in his creation and the measure of his care for each creature. Suffering that is merely shared cannot sustain significance and meaning; it soon degenerates into sympathy. One ought not to understate the import of "alongsideness," but neither ought one to assume that it exhausts the quality of God's suffering.

It is surely significant that the early Christian community

brought together the metaphors of Messiah and Suffering Servant: "The One who suffers the suffering of men is the One who has the passion, vision, and power of human liberation." [74] Yet the "suffering with" of God is different from the "suffering with" of man. This is not to divorce them but to argue that the quality of the experience can be differentiated. When the One who "suffers with" relates to the present as the power of the future, the promise of ultimate victory and of a truly new future is assured. Expectation replaces endurance. One suffers, then, not under the threat of hopelessness and futurelessness but under the promise of possibilities that man otherwise has no right to anticipate. The faithfulness of God to his visions of fulfillment and his promises of liberation save the sufferer from being a lonely figure in an oppressing world. "If one looks from the future of God into the godless and godforsaken present, the cross becomes the present form of the resurrection." [75] In man love taking the form of suffering yields comfort; in God love taking the form of suffering assures final triumph. The union of love and pain eventuates in power.

The suffering of God can also be understood as a function of the fact that he cannot make peace with what is. He who has the future as his mode of being lives and moves in contradiction to the present conditions. While it could be said that the suffering of man is often the consequence of his hopelessness, the suffering of God is a function of hope. When God works from his future into the present, it puts him in a state of tension; the promises are at odds with the realities. Jürgen Moltmann writes of this in the context of man's participation in the dynamics of hope: "Those who hope in Christ can no longer put up with reality as it is, but begin to suffer under it, to contradict it. Peace with God means conflict with the world, for the goad of the promised future stabs inexorably into the flesh of every unfulfilled present." [76]

Suffering eventuates in the being of God as his future engages the present; the cross stands guard over the truth of that. He who brings the future suffers the consequences of the present's resistance. Everything that is strives to sustain the "now" and preserve the advantages it affords. But God challenges the *status quo*. The God of the coming Kingdom disrupts the confidently settled conditions of the present and drives them against their will to a new day. God works against all the forces that deny man his future and his freedom; he is a suffering God because the powers of the present resist the power of the future. Pain in his own being is the consequence of his challenge to the dehumanizing and defuturizing conditions in existence. God suffers because political powers foreclose on the future for man; he suffers because man fears the future and makes peace with the present. But the willingness to be the suffering God against the forces of repression also constitutes the hope of liberation; because God cannot make peace with the present, he is the ground of hope for the future.

There is a dimension of the suffering God that ought not to escape us: the persuasiveness of the divine risk and its consequences. Dietrich Bonhoeffer understood this when he wrote from a prison camp: "God allows himself to be edged out of the world and on to the cross. God is weak and powerless in the world, and that is exactly the way, the only way, in which he can be with us and help us. . . . It is not by his omnipotence that Christ helps us, but by his weakness and suffering." [77] There are places suffering can reach and conditions it can affect that are inaccessible to the more direct forms of power. Words such as "contagion" and "infectious" only begin to suggest what happens when God opens himself to man in history and invites the cross with all its ongoing extensions in time. Suffering discloses God as nothing else save the triumph that ensues "on the third day." And Easter is not a way out but a way back into the suffering of God in and with the world. The God who comes to us from the future does not escape after one display but suffers on as he strives for his own fulfillment, not apart from history but within it. And that suffering makes him believable even as his resurrection makes him trustable. It communicates the anguish of his own Spirit. Then one can know that love is for real and commitment is complete.

The integrity of God's being for man is assured in his vulner-

ability; only One who suffers can help because only he has become one with man. Its persuasiveness is witnessed in the
human response it constructs. If nothing else, it reduces resistance to the future and its demands. And all the time one
knows that nothing demanded the suffering of God, save the
quality of his love. It not only makes liberation possible, it
makes the promise of liberation credible. Suffering is the incarnate form of the future in a loveless world; in it God authenti-
cates himself.

An uncomfortable question emerges from the understanding
of a suffering God: Does suffering affect the nature of the
deity, does it cause a difference in the nature of God? Certainly when man suffers, he is changed by the experience. Some
who argue from a base in process theology affirm that in the
most radical sense God is affected by his suffering in the world.
"The frustration experienced by the creatures of the cosmic
process may be spoken of as the wounds of God. The evils
springing from finite freedom and the evil springing from the
destructive . . . interactions . . . disrupt the harmony of God's
being. . . . God experiences . . . damages to his body in such
a way as to qualify the total situation within which the divine
purpose is henceforth carried on." [78] God is said to be not only
touched by his participation in suffering but in some degree
changed by it. Suffering "happens to him" in such a way as to
cause reformulation of his purposes, and alterations in his becoming. But that will not square with an understanding of
God whose reality is in the future. He is not now what he will
be. In his coming into existence he brings man and the world
along with him in the power of the future. But, as was argued
earlier, his coming into being is not a function of the past or
present but of the future. It is only the future that affects God.
The movement of God toward himself in the world necessi-
tates suffering; but it does not have a consequent effect on
what he becomes. God may be said to be disturbed but not dis-
rupted by suffering. Unlike man, he takes suffering into his
being without being altered by it. The future alters the suffering and not the reverse.

What does it mean for us that God is understood as suffering? No one needs to read Albert Camus to experience the absurdity of existence. No one needs to study the rhetoric of the black community and the third world to be informed about what hope has to work against. The cry for liberation rises both from the ghetto and the country club, from the General Motors assembly line and the board room, from the hospital room and from the health spa. The powerful and privileged may only whimper in their sleep while the politically and economically oppressed wail, but the anguish of futurelessness is no less real. Some allow themselves to be domesticated and make their peace with things as they are; resisting the impulse to hope, they become comfortable with hopelessness. In doing that, they allow themselves to be dehumanized. But the more sturdy ones struggle for vision and the courage to live in it. For the Christian, hope not only is understood in terms of what God did in Christ but is secured in it confidently. The suffering God is the hope of man. Confidence is not a function of our hoping either in the strength of some memories or of some dreams. Generations have paid for that in despair and disillusionment. The hope of faith stands on "the faithfulness of God to his vision and passion for the future of liberation." [79] And its credibility is elevated in the recognition of a God who suffers with us, for us, and because of us.


## Conditioned by the Future

It is the destiny of man in every age to determine the manner in which he will keep faith with the suffering God. This raises the issue of life-style. The word which specifies the essential quality of that is "proleptic." It means an error in chronology, something said to be occurring before its time. The proleptic life-style is one of living as if anticipated conditions were in force, living from hope rather than the present realities or projections based upon them. What is true for the person lies in the future, but he acts in the present on terms whose reality is yet to be.

What surfaces in the proleptic life-style is not the calculation of consequences but the attempt to inaugurate the future, not apprehension over the risks of the moment but concern with the verity of one's vision, not merely suffering under the present conditions but suffering against them. Conditioning is from the future. And behavior is more a function of visions than vicissitudes, more of images of the future than patterns from the past, more of hopes than happenstances. To take the future into one's life rather than to take one's life into the future is to live by realities that do not now exist as if they did. The terms of one's life are not legitimated by the societies of men but by the horizon exposed in Jesus of Nazareth. In living proleptically, one honors the promises of God by attempting to implement them in present decisions. And that means to put one's life on the line and in the line of the liberating action of God in Christ.

To be conditioned by the future involves a willingness to experience discontinuity. God, as the power of the future suffering in the present, calls man out of the security and safety of the familiar. Abraham had to leave behind his kindred and his land for he knew not where with only the promises of God as a basis for confidence. Loyalty to those promises meant that he was disconnected from earthly sources of security. He was, in one sense, cut off not only from the past but from its orderly development into a cautious future as well. In his homeland, existence was controlled and change managed in a way that was neither disruptive nor disconcerting. That stability he forfeited. The lines of Don Paolo in Silone's *Bread and Wine,* however, stand in support of the risk: "One must not be afraid, one must not be obsessed with the idea of security, even of the security of one's own virtue. Spiritual life and secure life do not go together." [80] It is the destiny of the faithful to risk exposure to existence in all its precariousness.

Yet the experience of discontinuity is not the negation of

the past. Memory and hope are too integrally related for that. What is negated is the past as an enclave to which one may retreat, or as a secure base from which projections may be made. To risk living from the future is to be deprived of the comfort of the familiar and predictable. And the freedom to risk new life comes from the realization that the only authentic security is from the future, and as one trusts it, anxiety is reduced. In the freedom that loyalty to the future promises, spontaneity is restored and a willingness to take risks is established. Discontinuity is not the denial of the past but an affirmation of the future of which it was once a function as well.

## The Expansion of Horizon

One impact on the person of the suffering God is an expansion of his horizon. The present sense of what is possible is always being overcome by a sense of indeterminate possibilities. When one accepts the priority of the future, the present is experienced as exploding in unpredictable directions. Man's ossified consciousness is converted into an anticipating consciousness; the sense of constriction is transformed into a sense of expectancy. In the proleptic life-style, one does not try to live with patient dignity before inevitable odds in a foreclosure of the future, but in confidence that the One who is the power of the future will bring about an utterly new event. Faith is not a mechanism for accommodation, but "the assurance of things hoped for, the conviction of things not seen" (Heb. 11:1). With the expansion of horizon, things as yet "not seen" begin to act upon the things that are seen. The effect of hope is to enable man to cope with existence in a way that holds open every conceivable option, including those which are inconceivable! To be conditioned by the future is to experience an expansion of horizon beyond anything the present can support, and forever to anticipate a new ingredient in one's existence.

In the proleptic life-style, imagination and fantasy play an integral role. The expansion of horizon occurs ultimately in the power of the future but more immediately through the production of images and the creation of visions. Imagination is essential to the practice of hope. Anticipation and expectancy are not self-sustaining phenomena; they come into being and are supported by a lively imagination that is not bound by present formations. Indeed, it is in "riding his imagination [that] man goes ahead of the existing conditions of the present." [81] The future is mediated through the exercise of imagination. Conversely, the death of imagination is an indication of futurelessness. It is in the images, symbols, and visions of the future that the existing order is broken open and made receptive to new possibilities. Change in the social order is dependent upon the presence of anticipations of the future that have not been strangled in advance by the question of feasibility.

New social orders are created from visions of men free to dream without the constriction of so-called realism. Realism that is governed by the future, rather than stultified by the past, fixes on the limitless sense of possibility. It is not limited by what may grow out of present facts, but it reaches for facts that are not now present. Feasibility and factuality are the enemies of hope; in the measure that they define realism, realism is the instrument of futurelessness. Yet it is crucial to bear in mind that imagination is in large measure a function of memory. Rubem Alves specifies the relationship when he writes that "memory . . . generates imagination. . . . Theological language is based on memory. It is a recital of that which happened in history. It tells about freedom making man open for the future and the future open for man." [82] It is not that what we imagine is derived from memory so that the future is a rerun on the past, but that the dynamic of hope and its consequences are reappropriated.

When Martin Luther King spoke of his "dreams," he specified conditions that nothing in the present could support as realistic. But in the process of dreaming, he remembered the tradition of the nation and the faith. The night before he was assassinated, King spoke of Moses and the prospect that he too might not reach the promised land. He remembered the way in which Moses and the Israelites set out with only the promise that God would be before them, and through that memory King was able to dream dreams that realism would have strangled. In his life, memory generated imagination; imagination reawakened the memory.

Yet imagination under the impact of the suffering God is more than the production of images. It may also translate into symbolic acts. Political fantasy requires not only the imagining of new forms of social existence but the embodiment of visions in one's existence. One's life is an image through which the presence of the future can be communicated. The function of visions is not only to be acted upon but to be acted out. In the most real sense the future can be taken into one's behavior. Hopes and visions, as they contradict the present, can be dramatized. The issues raised by the future can be formulated with one's life.

The fact that imagination creates freedom in a society where it does not exist means that a man may decide to live and act symbolically in order to point up the presence of the future. That was certainly the intent of the Berrigan brothers when participating in the burning of draft cards. Speaking in the Germantown section of Philadelphia, Daniel Berrigan said: "Dear Friends, how do we translate in our lives the bombing of helpless cities? How do we translate in our lives the millions of Vietnamese peasants perishing? How do we translate to the truth of our lives the 100,000 villages burned? . . . How do we translate on this summer morning the 50,000 American dead?" [83] They had answered those questions by the symbolic act of burning draft folders under the notion that it was better to burn paper than children. Not simply the words of the Berrigans but their lives have become the message. They not only moved into the future but moved on it in such a way as to raise for us the issue of the death of innocent children. And the impact of that cannot be readily discounted. Berrigan's own words on another occasion stand guard over that: "Now, when a man consents to live and die for the truth, he sets in motion spiritual rhythms whose outward influences are, in the nature of things, immeasurable. . . . The point is that others would come to a deepened consciousness: that their sense of existence and human issues would be sharpened to the point where they would 'do their thing'—a good thing, a human thing." [84] When one takes into his life the realities of his time, he effects awareness in others that enables them to respond in their own ways.

### Compromise and Joy

The proleptic life-style raises into view the issue of compromise. Those who call for realism gravitate to solutions that are approximations of hope. Indeed, the wise man is perceived to be the one who knows when to give ground. But the gospel is not about wise men but about "fools for Christ." Moderation, harmony, and accommodation are not Christian ideals; they do not square with the image of a suffering God. The cross neutralizes them; the expediency that leads to compromise is an anathema to Jesus of Nazareth.

Perhaps it will be helpful to make a discrimination in the usages of the word. "It is one thing to talk of compromise in the sense of flexibility and cooperation, a willingness to live with the ambiguities of life, to be aware of our questionable motives and imperfect actions, to reject dogmatism; and it is quite another thing to talk of selling out, retreating, being less than faithful, basing decisions on expediency rather than faithfulness to one's commitment." [85] It is compromise in the second sense that we are rejecting, the breeding of ambiguity with expediency that translates into contentment with tolerable solutions. Loyalty to hope requires that a man or group of men risk being rather absolute about their anticipations. When one is reckoning with the presence of the future, he expects the unexpected and does not reach for the tension-reducing solution. Those who claim it is unrealistic to be so rigorous need to have realism redefined. As Moltmann writes: "Hope alone is to be called 'realistic,' because it alone takes seriously the possibilities with which all reality is fraught. It does not take things as they happen to stand or to lie, but as progressing, moving things with possibilities of change." [86] The argument that one must be realistic fails to grasp that reality is in the future rather than in present constellations. Living from the future means acting and anticipating in ways that have no place on terms the present defines, because their time has not yet come. But, in part, the future comes because men live on terms yet to be realized. Moses did not try to make a deal with Pharaoh but issued a demand for freedom. Jesus did not court the cross, but neither did he make any of the compromises that might have avoided it.

Those who live in hope cannot settle for a reasonable arrangement of present conditions; obedience to the future forbids those compromises that in the final analysis are no more than an affirmation of the *status quo* in slightly modified forms. "This does not mean that we refuse to accept partial goals. It does mean that we will not give up ultimate goals in order to achieve partial goals." [87] The absoluteness of the proleptic life-style lies in the fact that it does not look for a way out but a way into the future. And the price for that may indeed be high. Total commitment to the future not only rules out compromises but requires sacrifices. And that is what restricts the disposition to self-righteousness and pride. The determination to go all the way in behalf of the future exacts too high a price to translate into arrogance of manner or righteousness of spirit. Self-serving and self-gratification recede at the foot of a cross.

But the cross is followed by and understood through the resurrection. All foreclosures on the future are ultimately overcome. God breaks open the present and creates indeterminate possibilities. The proleptic life-style, then, is not grim; neither is it a matter of endurance. Living for what is to come and acting out of its coming is a source of joy. A life shaped by hope is joyful because it thrives on anticipation rather than adaptation. While hope is for the future, it occasions a new response to the present. It is not an other-worldly word Paul writes in Romans but one which exemplifies the way in which the power of the future transforms the present and makes possible celebration. "I consider that the sufferings of this present time are not worth comparing with the glory that is to be revealed to us. . . . The creation itself will be set free from its bondage to decay and obtain the glorious liberty of the children of God. . . . But we ourselves . . . groan inwardly as we wait for adoption as sons, the redemption of our bodies. For in this hope we were saved" (Rom. 8:18, 21, 23, 24). What Paul hopes for does not exist; decay and groaning exist; but reality is in the future and presses in upon the present, calling forth a response of rejoicing.

The liberating action of God, yet to come but proleptically present, occasions celebration. With an eschatological horizon the Christian yearns for the "not yet" even as he rejoices in the present gifts of the future. Christians are God's happy people; they sing and dance and laugh a lot. The future is a source of festivity. The promise of liberation and the experience of participating in its processes in history engender a festive spirit. It is the irony of faith that a Suffering God who calls men to suffer with him in the world provides the occasion for rejoicing. Thus the final word is: "Rejoice in the Lord always; again I will say, Rejoice. . . . The Lord is at hand" (Phil. 4:4-5).

# NOTES

1. Johannes B. Metz, "Religion and Society in the Light of Political Theology," in *The Future of Hope*, ed. by Walter H. Capps (Fortress Press, 1970), p. 136.
2. *Ibid.*
3. Ignazio Silone, *Bread and Wine* (Penguin Books, Inc., 1946), pp. 298-299.
4. James H. Cone, *Black Power and Black Theology* (The Seabury Press, Inc., 1969), p. 7.
5. Frederick Herzog, "Towards the Waiting God," in *The Future of Hope*, ed. by Frederick Herzog (Herder & Herder, Inc., 1970), p. 69.
6. Quoted in David Little, "The Social Gospel Revisited," in *The Secular City Debate*, ed. by Daniel Callahan (The Macmillan Company, 1966), p. 69.
7. Rosemary Radford Ruether, *The Radical Kingdom* (Harper & Row, Publishers, Inc., 1970), p. 202.
8. Dale Patrick, "Opening Niebuhrian Thought to the Left," *Christianity and Crisis*, Oct. 19, 1970, p. 213.
9. Metz, "Religion and Society in the Light of Political Theology," in Capps (ed.), *The Future of Hope*, p. 149.
10. Jürgen Moltmann, "Political Theology," *Theology Today*, April, 1971, p. 20.
11. Carl E. Braaten, *The Future of God* (Harper & Row, Publishers, Inc., 1969), p. 165.
12. Daniel Berrigan, *The Trial of the Catonsville Nine* (Beacon Press, Inc., 1970), p. 81. Copyright © 1970 by Daniel Berrigan, S.J. Reprinted by permission of Beacon Press.

13. Rubem A. Alves, A Theology of Human Hope (Corpus Books, 1969), p. 3.
14. Johannes B. Metz, "Creative Hope," in New Theology, No. 5, ed. by Marty and Peerman (The Macmillan Company, 1969), p. 140.
15. Ernst Bloch, Man on His Own (Herder & Herder, Inc., 1971), p. 61.
16. Harvey Cox, On Not Leaving It to the Snake (The Macmillan Company, 1964), p. xiv.
17. Alves, op. cit., p. 114.
18. Carl E. Braaten, "The Future as the Source of Freedom," Theology Today, Jan., 1971, pp. 392-393.
19. Jürgen Moltmann, "Hope and History," Theology Today, Oct., 1968, p. 378.
20. Bloch, Man on His Own, p. 116.
21. Jürgen Moltmann, "Politics and the Practice of Hope," The Christian Century, March 11, 1970, p. 290.
22. William Stringfellow, "Jesus as Criminal," Christianity and Crisis, June 8, 1970, p. 119.
23. Ibid., p. 122.
24. Alves, op. cit., p. 111.
25. Ibid., p. 112.
26. Jürgen Moltmann, The Theology of Hope (Harper & Row, Publishers, Inc., 1967), p. 21.
27. Carl Braaten and Robert Jenson, The Futurist Option (Paulist/ Newman Press, 1970), p. 51.
28. J. A. T. Robinson, Jesus and His Coming (London: SCM Press, Ltd., 1957), p. 9.
29. Wolfhart Pannenberg, Theology and the Kingdom of God, ed. by Richard John Neuhaus (The Westminster Press, 1969), p. 52.
30. Ernst Bloch, Das Prinzip Hoffnung (Frankfurt/Main: Suhrkamp Verlag, 1959), Vol. I, p. 332.
31. Jürgen Moltmann, Religion, Revolution, and the Future (Charles Scribner's Sons, 1969), p. 149.
32. Ibid., p. 154.
33. Braaten and Jenson, op. cit., p. 77.
34. Jürgen Moltmann, "Theology as Eschatology," in The Future of Hope, ed. by Frederick Herzog (Herder & Herder, Inc., 1970), p. 10.

35. Pannenberg, op. cit., p. 63.
36. Moltmann, Religion, Revolution, and the Future, p. 135.
37. Braaten and Jenson, op. cit., pp. 84-85.
38. Carl E. Braaten, op. cit., p. 73.
39. Richard John Neuhaus, "Wolfhart Pannenberg: Profile of a Theologian," in Pannenberg, op. cit., p. 40.
40. Moltmann, Religion, Revolution, and the Future, p. 120.
41. Pannenberg, op. cit., p. 61.
42. Moltmann, Religion, Revolution, and the Future, p. 121.
43. Braaten, loc. cit., p. 385.
44. Alves, op. cit., p. 93.
45. Bloch, Man on His Own, pp. 161-162.
46. Ibid., p. 60.
47. James H. Cone, A Black Theology of Liberation (J. B. Lippincott Company, 1970), p. 11.
48. Ibid., p. 124.
49. Miles J. Jones, "Toward a Theology of the Black Experience," The Christian Century, Sept. 16, 1970, p. 1091.
50. Cone, A Black Theology of Liberation, p. 122.
51. Richard Dickinson, "So Who Needs Liberation?" The Christian Century, Jan. 13, 1971, p. 43.
52. Alves, op. cit., p. 76.
53. S. G. F. Brandon, Jesus and the Zealots (Charles Scribner's Sons, 1967), p. 1.
54. Oscar Cullmann, Jesus and the Revolutionaries (Harper & Row, Publishers, Inc., 1970), pp. 7-11.
55. Ibid., pp. 34-35.
56. Walter Wink, "Jesus and Revolution," Union Seminary Quarterly Review, Fall, 1969, p. 59.
57. Ibid.
58. Peter Berger, A Rumor of Angels (Doubleday & Company, Inc., 1969), p. 8.
59. Karl Barth, Deliverance to the Captives (Harper & Row, Publishers, Inc., 1961), p. 115.
60. Robinson, op. cit., p. 83.
61. Johannes B. Metz, quoted in The Power to Be Human, Charles C. West (The Macmillan Company, 1971), p. 250.
62. Albert Camus, Resistance, Rebellion, and Death (London: Hamish Hamilton, Ltd., 1961), pp. 50-51.

63. Pannenberg, *op. cit.*, p. 85.
64. James H. Cone, "Black Consciousness and the Black Church," *Christianity and Crisis*, Nov. 2 and 16, 1970, p. 248.
65. Alves, *op. cit.*, pp. 120-122.
66. Dietrich Bonhoeffer, *Ethics* (The Macmillan Company, 1955), p. 21.
67. Moltmann, *The Theology of Hope*, p. 338.
68. Braaten, *op. cit.*, p. 121.
69. *Ibid.*, pp. 119-120.
70. *Ibid.*, pp. 123-124.
71. Cox, *op. cit.*, p. 143.
72. Alves, *op. cit.*, p. 145.
73. Daniel Day Williams, *The Spirit and the Forms of Love* (Harper & Row, Publishers, Inc., 1968), p. 167.
74. Alves, *op. cit.*, p. 118.
75. Moltmann, "Theology as Eschatology," in Herzog (ed.), *The Future of Hope*, p. 31.
76. Moltmann, *The Theology of Hope*, p. 21.
77. Dietrich Bonhoeffer, *Prisoner for God* (The Macmillan Company, 1953), p. 164.
78. Kenneth Cauthen, *Science, Secularization, and God* (Abingdon Press, 1969), p. 215.
79. Alves, *op. cit.*, p. 119.
80. Silone, *op. cit.*, p. 299.
81. Rubem A. Alves, "Program for Ethics," *Union Seminary Quarterly Review*, Winter, 1971, p. 159.
82. *Ibid.*, p. 167.
83. Daniel Berrigan, "Things Hoped For," *Christianity and Crisis*, Sept. 21, 1970.
84. Daniel Berrigan, *No Bars to Manhood* (Bantam Books, Inc., 1971), p. 47.
85. Arthur G. Gish, *The New Left and Christian Radicalism* (Wm. B. Eerdmans Publishing Company, 1970), p. 95.
86. Moltmann, *The Theology of Hope*, p. 25.
87. Gish, *op. cit.*, p. 111.